Cook Book

COOK BOOK

BY MRS. E. F. WARREN

NEW

SOUTHERN

RECIPES

—2—

©CLA659764

SOUPS

OYSTER SOUP—One quart of sweet milk, let come to a boil, add one heaping tablespoonful butter and salt to taste, two dozen oysters, let boil in a little water or liquor in a different vessel; when both come to a boil pour them together, put a few oyster crackers in bottom of soup plate and serve soup on them very hot, with a little black pepper, take more milk and oysters it for a crowd.

CREAM OF TOMATO SOUP—One quart of milk, one can of tomatoes, press tomatoes through a collander, add a pinch of soda to prevent curdling, let milk come to a boil then add tomatoes; season with salt and pepper. Thicken with one tablespoonful of butter rubbed into flour. Serve with toasted bread This soup when done should be thick as cream

CREAM OF ASPARAGUS SOUP—Take a can of asparagus tips and boil thoroughly and press through a collander, have ready one quart of boiling milk to which add the asparagus pulp, season with salt and pepper to taste, thicken with a lump of butter and little flour, add two tablespoonfuls of cream, serve hot with toasted crackers.

CHICKEN CONSOMME—Cut a fowl into pieces, cover with cold water, add one cup of rice, and boil until thoroughly cooked, remove the chicken, when cool, skim off the grease, strain, pressing the rice through the sieve, add to the liquor an equal amount of cream, season very highly with salt and cayenne pepper, reheat and serve very hot in cups with spoonful of whipped cream over each.

CHICKEN GUMBO—Fry very brown a large tender chicken, take upon a dish and fry in the gravy one quart of sliced okra, add to chicken, put chicken and okra in porcelain vessel of cold water, add one large onion fried in gravy, one spoon of butter, two sliced Irish potatoes, one can of tomatoes, one spoonful of rice, add six crackers, salt to taste and let cook for several hours, being careful not to scorch, add one tablespoonful of black pepper when ready to come up

VEGETABLE SOUP—Fill pot about half full of cold water, put either a beef bone or left-over broiled steak into the water, then cut up three Irish potatoes, about one pint of okra or more, one tablespoonful butter, put in a skillet and cut up and fry one onion in the butter, pour one can of tomatoes in with onions and chicken with a little flour, after frying them pour into the other mixture; when nearly done add a tablespoonful of rice and spaghetti broken in small bits, salt and pepper to taste.

MEATS

HAMBERGER STEAK—Take a nice sized steak and grind, season with salt, red pepper and a tiny bit of onion, fry in little cakes like sausages until brown, then make a thickened gravy and pour one can of tomatoes into it then pour your little cakes all into the gravy and let cook awhile; serve hot on a dish with gravy poured over steak.

OLD FASHIONED FRIED STEAK (FRENCH STYLE)—Beat a steak thoroughly with hatchet, have one spoonful of lard or two of cooking oil hot in skillet; cover steak good with flour on both sides and put in hot grease; let brown on both sides, then make a gravy by putting some dry flour in hot grease to brown, with one teacup of cold water and a little onion, salt and pepper; put steak back into gravy and cook a good while, turning steak over from side to side. Add one can of tomatoes when gravy is first made and cook steak in it.

BROILED STEAK—Take a nice piece of steak and beat thoroughly with hatchet, wipe top of stove off perfectly clean, grease steak on both sides and throw on top of stove and turn over rapidly until as done as wanted. Take up, place on dish and sprinkle salt and black pepper over it and cut up cold butter, about a tablespoonful over steak, and run dish in top of stove until butter melts, then take out, turn over in butter gravy and serve at once on hot dish Never wash steak that is to be broiled Wipe with damp cloth.

BROILED CHICKEN—Take a small chicken, dress and wash clean, dry with cloth, have a very hot baker on top of stove. Salt and pepper to taste, put chicken on baker and cover with a tablespoonful of butter, put flat top on

—8—

chicken and set a heavy iron on top; don't cook too fast; turn often until done.

BAKED CHICKEN—Cook an old chicken tender, kill and dress the day before, rub a little soda over the outside. lay fowl in ice box over night, before cooking wash off all the soda and grease fowl all over, then put in roasting pan with about two inches of water in bottom, and cover tight, cook until it begins to tender, take out and fill with dressing. Turn often and baste with water in pan until brown and tender.

DRESSING FOR BAKED CHICKEN—Take a pan of egg bread made of corn meal and some light bread or biscuits, pour water over to soften; mix thoroughly, season with salt and pepper to taste, tablespoonful of butter or lard, one onion cut small, a little celery and two raw eggs, put into skillet, with little grease on top of stove and let cook awhile then remove and stuff fowl with it.

SOUTHERN STYLE FRIED CHICKEN—Take a young chicken, dress and cut up in small pieces, roll in flour, season to taste with salt and black pepper Have a skillet with very hot grease, put chicken in and fry to a crisp brown, take chicken out and make a cream gravy as follows: Sprinkle dry flour in grease and brown, pour one cup of sweet milk, add salt and pepper to taste, stir constantly and don't burn, till thick as wanted.

CHICKEN STEW—Take a large chicken, dress and cut up and boil until tender in half a pot of water, make dumplings as follows One pint of flour, one heaping tablespoonful of lard, one level teaspoonful of salt, make up with ice water to a stiff dough, roll thin and cut into small pieces; put in pot with chicken and a spoonful of butter; take half a cup of cold water, thicken with flour and pour in pot to thicken gravy; sprinkle with salt and pepper to taste.

CHICKEN PIE—Dress and boil one chicken in about half gallon of water until tender, then make a crust as follows: One pint of flour, two heaping tablespoonfuls of lard, one level teaspoonful of salt, make stiff dough with ice water; roll thin crust large enough to cover the bottom of pan; then put chicken and liquor in pan, salt and pepper to taste; put in one cup of butter one cup of sweet milk, sift a little flour over the mixture, cut some of the dough into small pieces and put all around among the chicken, then roll a thin crust and put over top of pan; let middle of the crust go down on the mixture, bring up on sides and press down with a fork on the edge of the pan. Puncture the top of the crust with a fork, putting pieces of butter into puncture, set in stove and brown slowly.

BEEF (POT ROAST)—Put small roast in pot on top of stove with small quantity of water; cook until brown, then season to taste with salt and pepper sprinkle well with flour, pour tablespoonful of vinegar over meat; keep pot tightly covered, turn roast often; when nearly done pour in one can of tomatoes and let cook a good while.

STUFFED ROAST—Put roast in roasting pan, put some flour, salt and pepper and two tablespoons of vinegar over same, put a little water in roasting pan and keep covered tightly. Make dressing like for baked chicken. When roast is nearly done slash down the roast and put dressing in slashes, let brown nicely; cook for three or four hours till perfectly tender.

BEEF HASH—Cut up beef in small pieces, one Irish potato and a small onion; put in stew pan with a little water; let boil until tender; put a little flour into it to thicken the gravy.

FRIED BEEF HASH—Grind cold roast or any kind of cold beef, add one small ground onion, small quantity of cooked Irish potatoes, salt to season, adding a pinch of red pepper, make into small cakes like sausages and fry in hot grease.

PORK ROAST AND POTATOES—Take a nice pork roast, wash and put in roasting pan, put salt and pepper and flour over same, fill pan about half full of water and keep well basted; when about half done turn the skin side up and slash deep, and let brown; when about half done peel a lot of small sweet potatoes and put around roast and let them all brown together; cook two or three hours or until tender; serve potatoes around roast on dish.

PORK SAUSAGE—Take pork, lean and fat, grind in meat chopper, season with salt and red and black pepper to taste; take a little sage and dry in stove; rub through sifter and into meat; mix all thoroughly; make into small cakes and fry.

BACK-BONE AND DUMPLINGS—Take the back-bone of a hog, cut into small pieces, or as much as needed; put on in pot of water, boil together until tender; lift out of pot and make dumplings as directed in chicken stew; put on in pot of water where bone has boiled; thicken gravy and salt and pepper to taste; when done put back-bone in with stew and serve all together

PORK SPARE RIBS—Take ribs from side, cut across several times, put in roasting pan with water to cover, sprinkle flour, salt and pepper over meat, cover and put in stove and cook until tender.

BROILED QUAIL ON TOAST—Dress and wash clean, have a hot baker on stove; salt and pepper to taste; tablespoon of butter rubbed over quail, put a top over it and a heavy weight to hold it down, turn often and cook slowly until done, but not dry; brown two slices of bread nicely; pour melted butter over pieces and serve between bread.

SQUIRREL FRIED—Take a squirrel, cut in small pieces, put in vessel of water and boil till tender, take out and roll thoroughly in flour; season with salt and black pepper; have skillet of hot grease and fry till brown; take out and make a nice brown gravy; return squirrel to gravy and let cook in that for a while

BAKED HAM—Take Armour ham, wash and scrape thoroughly; put ham on top of stove in roaster half full of cold water; let stay on top of stove till it begins to boil, then set in stove and let cook two or three hours, accord ing to size; keep tightly covered until done.

MEXICAN HASH—Cut into small pieces any cold meat, beef, veal or pork, add cold potatoes, bread crumbs, two onions, a little garlic, celery seed, red pepper, salt and black pepper to taste, a little butter, put into a skillet with a little hot lard; after cooking a while, add one can of tomatoes; let cook until thoroughly mixed and rather dry; serve hot on buttered toast. Be sure and have plenty of onions and pepper and it will be true Mexican style.

ROAST TURKEY—Dress nicely and put on ice all night, then wash and put in roasting pan (never boil), grease all over with lard, salt and pepper to taste, fill roasting pan about half full of water; put in stove and let cook slowly; keep tightly covered, baste often; when nearly done make a dressing as for baked chicken and stuff; if you like a few oysters may be added to dressing, when well done, serve on dish garnished with slices of hard boiled eggs, celery leaves arranged around dish

ASPARAGUS LOAF—Two tablespoons of butter, two of flour, four eggs, one scant tablespoon of gelatine, juice of one lemon, one can asparagus tips, one pint of whipped cream, salt and pepper to taste. Heat the butter and sift the flour into a little water and stir up and add to butter in double boiler Beat the eggs well and pour over them the butter mixture stirring the eggs constantly, put this again in a double boiler, cook until eggs are done, stirring constantly until leaving fire. Add dissolved gelatine, lemon juice and salt and pepper, when cool add four kitchen spoons of whipped cream. Line molds with asparagus tips and pour in the custard putting asparagus layer on top Set on ice to congeal and serve with mayonnaise.

—12—

CREOLE CHICKEN—One chicken, one onion, one can tomatoes, one can mushrooms, one green pepper, salt and pepper to taste. Boil chicken tender and then cut in pieces

SAUCE FOR THE CHICKEN—Cut the onion into small pieces and fry in butter until yellow using a skillet, cut into this one green pepper, one can tomatoes, one can mushrooms, salt and pepper to taste, one teaspoon Worcestershire, one teaspoon sugar. Cook this mixture until thoroughly done, then add chicken; cover and let cook until well seasoned.

SPANISH MEAT BALLS—Grind with meat chopper one pound of raw beef, then chop a tablespoon of onions, add a cup full of bread crumbs dried and ground, black pepper and salt and one raw egg. Mix thoroughly and roll into balls. Put about three tablespoons of fat or oil of any kind in frying pan and fry a medium size onion in it Take about one can of tomatoes and press through a collander and put on stove and stew until thick, about an hour. Fry your meat balls after adding a little onion. Salt and pepper and some parsley, then stew them in sauce about an hour If sauce gets too thick add hot water

CREOLE OYSTERS—One can tomato soup, one green pepper, one-half small onion, one stick of celery. one tablespoon flour, two of butter; put butter in bottom of spider, add onion, when brown add flour and pepper, then slow cook until thick, season highly with salt and pepper It is best to boil green peppers ten minutes before cutting fine. Drain medium sized oysters, put layer in pan, cover layer with Creole sauce and sprinkle with cracker crumbs. Fill pan in this order and run in stove for a few minutes. This is a delicious dish

CHICKEN RISSOLES—One cup finely chopped chicken will make six rissoles Mix with chicken twelve finely chopped stuffed olives, salt, pepper and onions to taste. With your largest biscuit cutter cut from rich pie crust twelve rounds. On six of these put a spoon of the chicken mixture, lay the other six rounds on these, wet the edges with cold water and press firmly together with a fork. Fry brown in deep fat. They may be dipped in egg and bread crumbs before frying and they will puff up.

GOULASH—Fry out two large slices of salt pork. Season one pound of hamburger steak with half teaspoon of salt, a generous dash of pepper, add one onion minced, crackers rolled, add two tablespoons of water to moisten. Form into small balls and fry brown in the pork fat. Break one-fourth package of macaroni and boil until tender. Butter two-quart pan. Put in layer of macaroni, seasoning with a dash of salt and pepper, then a layer of the meat cakes, using the fat they were fried in, then another layer of macaroni. Pour over the whole one-half can of tomatoes, cover and place on back of stove and let simmer for two hours but be careful not to scorch.

FISH

BAKED RED SNAPPER (DELICIOUS)—Take a red snapper and fill the inside with dressing made by recipe as given for baked chicken, then pour a can of tomatoes, half a cup of tomato catsup, two tablespoons of Worcestershire sauce, one tablespoonful of butter, salt and pepper to taste, sprinkle flour over all and add a little water; baste often, and cook about three-quarters of an hour. Bake inside of stove; serve with sliced lemon over the fish.

BAKED CATFISH—Wash and dry fish and lay in pan; fill pan about half full of water; lay slices of fat bacon on top; butter may be used in place of bacon; when thoroughly done and brown, thicken gravy and serve with dressing as follows: Beat yolks of two eggs with two tablespoonsful of cream, one teaspoon of mustard, one-half cup of vinegar, boil together until thick. Beat whites stiff and beat into sauce and serve cold over fish

FISH DRESSING NO. 2—Moisten bread crumbs with melted butter, season with chopped pickle, lemon juice, a trace of powdered herbs, salt and pepper, add a little cold water if needed.

FISH CHOWDER—Cut in half one dozen medium sized perch or trout, one dozen Irish potatoes peeled and sliced, one dozen sliced or one can of tomatoes, one pound of fat sliced bacon, season with salt and pepper and Worcestershire sauce, one cup of butter, one dozen onions, sliced thin; cover the bottom of pan with a layer of bacon, then a layer of fish, potatoes, onions, a layer of tomatoes, then a layer of bacon, fish, etc, until it is all in the pan, then add sauce and a little water; cover closely and cook slowly for three hours on top of stove. Do not stir; lift from pan with a ladle. Do not break more than necessary. Lessen the quantity of everything in proportion for a small family. This is very fine.

BOILED SALMON WITH SAUCE—Drop unopened can of salmon into a pot of water and boil for one hour.

SAUCE FOR SAME—Three hard boiled eggs; take the yolks and rub into them one teaspoonful of mustard, a little salt and red pepper; one-quarter pound of melted butter, juice of one lemon and chopped whites of the eggs; just before serving open can of salmon and pour liquor into sauce. Serve salmon with creamed Irish potatoes.

OYSTER COCKTAIL—Two dozen oysters or more; put half cup of tomato catsup, two tablespoons of Worcestershire sauce, juice of a lemon, salt and red pepper to taste, one teaspoon of vinegar. Thoroughly chill before serving.

STUFFED CRABS—One large can of crabs, six soda crackers; roll fine; two hard boiled eggs, one raw egg, tablespoon of butter, one cup of sweet milk; salt to taste; make pretty hot with red pepper; one teaspoonful of Worcestershire sauce, pinch of mustard; mix thoroughly; fill shells lightly, then sprinkle some of the rolled crackers over the top of each; set in stove and let brown. Serve hot with sliced lemon.

SCALLOPED FISH—Boil the fish and pick it fine; boil one pint of sweet milk with one onion; strain out the onion, put the milk on again; add one-quarter pound of butter with a very little flour stirred in. Season with pepper and salt to taste; let it boil to the consistency of very thick cream; put in baking dish by alternate layers of fish and cream; then add layer of cracker crumbs, butter salt and pepper, and the juice of one lemon; bake fifteen minutes.

SALMON BALLS—Remove the bones, salt and pepper to taste, make balls and roll in meal; fry in very hot lard till brown.

OYSTER CROQUETTES—One quart of oysters, one pint of chicken, a scant pint of bread crumbs, the yolk of two eggs, one tablespoonful of butter, salt and pepper to taste. Chop oysters and chicken very fine; soak bread crumbs in oyster liquid, then mix all ingredients and shape in cones; dip in egg and cracker crumbs and fry brown

OYSTER PATTIES—Take of oysters according to the number to be served and put them in the same pan with butter, pepper, salt, and a little flour; stir and let simmer for a few minutes on the stove; bake shells of rich puff paste in patty tins, also small rounds for covers and set in the oven for five minutes They should be served immediately.

OYSTER OMELET—Make a nice omelet and just before turning it over fill the center with oyster filling, prepared as for patties; asparagus and mushrooms can be used in the same manner.

BROILED OYSTERS—After paring crusts from six slices of bread, toast a rich brown and place on heated platter, put can with butter on back of stove where it will melt but not cook, drain and carefully wipe two dozen oysters. After seasoning with salt and pepper, drop on very hot griddle; turn almost instantly and quickly remove from griddle to sauce of melted butter; after the oysters are broiled, place four on each slice of toast; pour on the melted butter and serve hot.

CREAMED OYSTERS AND PEPPERS—Heat one quart of oysters to boiling point, drain and make a sauce of the liquor by adding cream, butter, flour, salt and pepper; add to the oysters. Cut stems out of peppers and remove seed; put oysters into these cases, sprinkle buttered cracker crumbs over top and brown Serve on toast

TROUT STUFFED AND FRIED MEXICAN STYLE—
Stuff the trout with cold cooked red fish, chopped mushrooms, bread crumbs, lemon juice and two well beaten eggs; dip fish in oil, then in bread crumbs and fry rich brown. Serve with tomato sauce and capers.

SALMON A LA REINE—Put into a frying pan a tablespoonful of butter; when melted stir in a tablespoonful of flour; make a smooth paste, then add a gill of water, one lemon, salt and pepper to taste, one small onion, minced fine, yolks of three hard boiled eggs mashed; then put in contents of one can of salmon and let simmer five minutes; cut whites in rings and place on salmon after it is in the dish. Good hot or cold

COD FISH BALLS—Take package of cod fish or as much as needed and boil in good deal of water; drain off and boil again in more water until tender. Pick all the bones out thoroughly, then mash up with as much boiled Irish potatoes as fish and season with black pepper; make into small cakes and drop into hot grease and fry till brown.

BREAD

WAFFLES NO. 2—One egg beaten separately, one cup butter milk, little salt, one-half teaspoonful soda, two teaspoons Royal Baking Powder, one heaping tablespoon of lard, flour enough to make batter just a little stiff.

MUFFINS—Two cups of flour, one cup of sweet milk, three tablespoonsful of sugar, pinch of salt, one egg, butter size of an egg, two tablespoonsful of Royal Baking Powder; cook in muffin tins.

SPOON BREAD—Three eggs, three cups buttermilk, one cup corn meal, one teaspoon soda, salt and a lump of butter; bake in a pan one-half hour.

CORN BREAD—One pint of meal, one level teaspoonful of salt, one level teaspoon of Royal Baking Powder, about a light half teaspoonful of soda, buttermilk enough to make a nice batter. First sift meal then put everything in, then pour a little boiling water on meal; put heaping spoon of grease in pan and let get hot; pour in mixture and bake.

BUTTERMILK BISCUIT—One quart flour, two heaping tablespoon lard, two teaspoons Royal Baking Powder, one-half teaspoon soda, mixed with flour, two teaspoons salt; mix with buttermilk; make rather stiff dough, roll thin; cut and place one on top of other and bake quickly.

SPOON BREAD No. 2—Use the real Southern corn meal and scald one and a half cups thoroughly; allow to stand till cool; beat three eggs separately, add yolks to three cups of milk, then stir in the meal; add half a teaspoonful of salt; melt a piece of butter the size of a walnut; add a teaspoon of Royal Baking Powder and the whites of eggs; turn into a buttered dish or pan and cook in a moderate oven for three-quarters of an hour, or until it is the consistency of a thick custard Send to table in the dish and serve with a spoon.

FLANNEL CAKES—Take one pint of flour and sift one full teaspoon of soda, one teaspoon Royal Baking Powder, sift with flour; add one heaping teaspoonful sugar, one level spoon salt, one and one-third pints of buttermilk, one egg. Beat all together well and have batter pretty thick, have griddle medium hot and grease with bacon rind

BEATEN BISCUITS—One quart flour, two ounces lard, one large teacup of sweet milk; mix into a stiff dough, beat or run through the machine for twenty or thirty minutes, till the dough blisters and is smooth. It may then be rolled and cut; stick with fork which should penetrate the board Bake in quick oven An additional ounce of butter will make a richer biscuit if desired

BUTTERMILK BISCUITS—One level teaspoon of soda, one level teaspoon of salt, one rounding teaspoon Royal Baking Powder, one large heaping tablespoon of lard, two cups fresh buttermilk; mix all together; work in flour to make soft dough; roll thin, cut with small cutter and bake in hot oven

A RECIPE FOR TWELVE MUFFINS—One tablespoon of butter, one of sugar, two eggs, one cup of milk, two cups flour, two teaspoons Royal Baking Powder; beat butter and sugar to a cream, beat eggs and add gradually, then add milk flour and Royal Baking Powder; mix well and divide into warm buttered muffin pans; bake in moderate oven for twenty minutes.

SALLIE LUNN—One quart of flour, one tablespoon salt, one teaspoon of sugar; rub in heaping tablespoon butter and lard mixed in equal parts, one boiled Irish potato mashed fine; make up dough with one-half teacup of yeast, two eggs well beaten, enough warm water to make consistency of lightbread dough; knead well, when it has risen put it lightly into a cake mold for the second rising when it has risen the second time bake in a moderately hot oven

BISCUITS—Two rounding teaspoons of Royal Baking Powder, one level teaspoon salt, one large heaping table-spoon of lard, about two-thirds of a pint of sweet milk; pour milk into other ingredients and add gradually flour enough to make a soft dough; roll out and cut with small cutter and bake in hot oven a few minutes before ready to serve

QUICK ROLLS—Sift three cups of flour into a bread bowl, make a hole in the center and put into it one tablespoon of lard or butter melted, one level teaspoon of salt, one cake of Fleischman's yeast, dissolve in half a cup of luke warm sweet milk; add the white of one egg well beaten; knead very little; put to rise for two hours, then make into rolls and let rise one hour, then bake; these can be made after breakfast and baked for luncheon. This quantity makes one goodsized pan of rolls.

DATE MUFFINS—Cream two tablespoons butter with one-quarter cup sugar; add two well beaten eggs, then one cup milk and two cups flour sifted with two tea-spoons Royal Baking Powder; beat thoroughly and add pinch of salt and one cup dates cut fine. Bake in quick oven. These make a delicious luncheon or supper dish.

DELICATE MUFFINS—Three cups of sifted flour, two teaspoons Royal Baking Powder, one level teaspoon salt, one egg, one pint of milk, two tablespoons melted Snow-drift lard; sift together the flour, salt and baking pow-der; add egg well beaten, then add milk and beat, then add melted Snowdrift lard; beat well and bake in hot greased muffin tins.

CINNAMON ROLLS—Put two tablespoons butter into one pint of flour, one teaspoon Royal Baking Powder, one-half teaspoon salt, two-thirds cup of milk; add one egg well beaten, mix lightly and roll into thin sheet; spread lightly with butter, dust over four or five tablespoons sugar and sprinkle with cinnamon, make into pocket-book rolls or roll and cut; let rise twenty minutes. This makes two dozen rolls.

WAFFLES—Make batter with one quart of flour, one quart sour milk, two eggs beaten separately, three tablespoons melted butter, one teaspoon soda and half teaspoon salt.

LIGHT ROLLS, FRENCH STYLE—Take one cake of Fleischman's yeast cake, dissolve in pint of warm water, one quart flour, two eggs, one cup sugar, tablespoon of lard, sift flour, add sugar and work lard into it and make into a stiff batter with the water the yeast cake has been dissolved in, put the eggs in batter and beat together thoroughly; season with salt to taste; put in warm place to rise till it is light and foamy, then add about a quart of flour to make a stiff dough; knead till smooth, then let rise again, then pinch off your rolls and place in pan without working; set in moderate hot stove and bake; before baking grease over the top of the bread, also grease your pan before putting bread in for baking.

POTATO ROLLS—Two cups mashed Irish potatoes, 1-2 cup ground meat, salt to taste, a dash of pepper, a few drops of onion juice, one tablespoon of parsley chopped fine, one egg, bread crumbs to mix.   Add salt, pepper, onion juice and a little of parsley to the mashed potatoes and a little cold milk.   Flatten out a spoonful of potatoes and take one spoon chopped meat, add salt, pepper and rest of parsley to meat, and put on potatoes and roll the potatoes around the meat, take raw and dip roll into same and bread crumbs and fry in hot fat.   Make rolls two and three inches long.

A GOOD ROLL—Cook well done, enough Irish potatoes to amount to one and half cups when run through ricer, dissolve one cake of yeast in one cup of tepid water, to the potatoes add two eggs beaten light, one half cup sugar, then the yeast. Add one cup flour, one of sweet milk alternately beating with egg whip. If necessary add more flour to make as thick as for batter cakes. Let rise twice its bulk in warm place free from drafts. Make into smooth dough with one quart flour, one heaping teaspoon salt and one cooking spoon of lard, in winter it takes batter about two hours to rise, in summer not so long. Roll out, make into small rolls and put in a greased pan, grease tops, cover, let rise about one hour and bake.

ROXBURY DROPS—Cream half cup sugar with quarter cup butter, stir in half cup of molasses and half cup sour milk. With this mix one and a half cups sifted flour, half teaspoon cloves, one of cinnamon and a little nutmeg, beat yolks of two eggs and add, stir in one-half cup seedless raisins, one-half cup chopped nuts rolled in a little flour, one teaspoon soda dissolved in little boiling water and last the whites stiffly beaten. The dough should be quite stiff, if necessary use little more flour. Drop by teaspoonfuls on a buttered tin leaving space between to spread, bake for fifteen or twenty minutes in a moderate oven.

CINNAMON ROLLS—Make a good biscuit dough either with Royal Baking Powder or soda and sour milk, roll one-half inch thick, spread liberally with butter and sprinkle with light brown sugar and sift cinnamon lightly over the sugar, roll up, beginning at one edge, moisten the edge so it will hold the roll, cut in slices about one and a half inches, stand on end and bake. These are fine to eat with coffee

PEANUT STRAWS—Make a nice rich pastry, roll it out and spread one-half with softened peanut butter, wet the edges of the crust and fold the remaining half over it. Roll lightly with a rolling pin and prick here and there with a fork to prevent puffing up. Cut in strips about one inch wide and three long, bake in a quick oven until lightly browned and brush over with sweet milk.

VEGETABLES

CORN FRITTERS—One can corn through meat grinder, measure a pint, add two eggs beaten, one teaspoon of butter, salt and pepper, one teaspoon sugar, one tablespoon of milk and. enough flour to make it possible to handle, make into little cakes, using as little flour as possible; drop into hot fat and fry deep brown. Serve very hot after draining.

BROILED EGG PLANT (MEXICAN STYLE)—Soak slices of egg plant in highly seasoned olive oil, using all kinds of herbs in it; broil slices on hot griddle and serve with tomato sauce.

ASPARAGUS WITH VINAIGRETTE DRESSING—Remove asparagus from can to platter, four tablespoons vinegar, salt and pepper to taste, three tablespoonsful of olive oil, little minced parsley, quarter of chopped onion, one quarter pint of olives, chopped fine, pinch of sugar.

SQUASH COOKED MEXICAN STYLE—Take baking dish or pan, tablespoon of grease, layer of raw sliced squash and layer of fresh sliced tomatoes, and a layer of onions; season with red pepper and salt; cut up one green pepper, repeat the layers until pan is nearly full; put in few pieces of butter over the whole, cover tight and cook in slow oven.

BEANS—String and put into a pot of boiling water with a piece of fat meat and boil for two hours or till well done. Salt to taste.

EGG PLANT—Slice and peel egg plant and put on to boil, water enough to cover, mash up and add a half cup of flour, for one eggplant add one egg, enough sweet milk to make a thick batter, salt to taste and use plenty of black pepper; put tablespoon of grease in skillet and get hot and make egg plant into small cakes and fry brown. Add more flour if needed

CAULIFLOWER—Trim off the outside leaves of a nice fresh cauliflower, tie up in a piece of cheese cloth and put into well salted boiling water. Boil for twenty or thirty minutes, being careful to take out as soon as tender or it will fall to pieces, drain and separate into little flowerettes, put in baking dish, pour over cream sauce, sprinkle thickly with grated cheese and brown in a quick oven. Omit cheese if desired

SPINACH—Pick and wash thoroughly, put in a little hot water and boil about half an hour, salt and pepper to taste, and pour melted butter over it and slice several hard boiled eggs over the whole

STUFFED IRISH POTATOES—Take as many medium-sized potatoes as needed, wash and bake whole with skins on, inside of stove, when done, cut off one end and take a small spoon and scoop out the inside without breaking the peeling, take the pulp of the potato, mix it up with sweet milk, salt and pepper to taste and a tiny bit of ground onion, a tablespoonful of butter, refill hulls with mixture and put back in stove with cut ends up and let brown. Serve hot in hulls

IRISH POTATO CHIPS—Take as many potatoes as needed, wash and peel and slice very thin on a potato slicer, then let stand in cold water while your skillet, half full of cooking oil or lard, is getting hot, then drain thoroughly and put just a few potatoes at a time in the pan and stir around lightly in grease until a light brown, then take out quickly before they get too brown; drain off grease thoroughly as you take them up. Serve hot with a little salt sprinkled over them. Never try to fry potatoes in salty grease, and never salt till ready to serve.

FRENCH FRIED POTATOES—Peel potatoes and slice in strips as big as your little finger. Stand in cold water for a while, then fry in hot grease until brown. Serve hot with a little salt sprinkled over them.

SQUASH—Boil whole, young, tender squash, mash up and fry in hot grease; season with salt, pepper, a little butter and chopped onion. Let fry down brown.

FRIED SWEET POTATOES—Peel and slice not too thin, pour boiling water, amount needed, over them with a handful of salt thrown into water; let stand a while then fry in moderate hot skillet till nicely brown.

SWEET POTATOES IN THE PAN—Slice as for frying, put in pan one cup or more of sugar according to amount of potatoes, one spoonful of butter and a good pinch of salt. Fill pan about half full of water, put in bottom of stove and let cook until syrup is thick and potatoes brown Serve hot in pan.

SWEET POTATO PONE—Grate a few potatoes, as much as needed, and add enough sugar to sweeten, two cups sweet milk, one-half cup butter and three eggs, little nutmeg. Bake slowly till thoroughly done.

ASPARAGUS ON TOAST—Take bread sliced thin and brown nicely, make a nice dressing of sweet milk, tablespoon of butter, salt and pepper to taste, and thicken with about half cup sifted flour, open can of asparagus tips, put into dressing and let come to a boil. Don't put asparagus into dressing until it gets thick. Serve about three or four pieces of asparagus on a piece of toast with dressing poured over. Serve hot.

MUSHROOMS—Open can and cook for a short while, and make a dressing just like asparagus and cook in that for a while.

BAKED TOMATOES—Take tomatoes, as many as people you have to serve, scoop out inside, chop up and mix with mushrooms, a few crackers rolled, one spoon of butter, salt and pepper to taste, replace in tomatoes, sprinkle a few cracker crumbs over tomatoes and a little melted butter and let brown.

STEWED TOMATOES—Take one can of tomatoes, pour into skillet one and a half cups of sugar, two cold biscuits crumbled up, one spoon of butter, salt to taste with a little black pepper, stew down until almost candy.

FRIED GREEN TOMATOES—Slice green tomatoes, salt and pepper some meal like you were going to fry fish, dip your tomatoes in meal and fry in hot grease Serve hot on flat dish

DEVILED TOMATOES—Take two or three large tomatoes not over-ripe, cut into slices half an inch thick, and lay on a sieve, make a dressing of one tablespoon of butter, one of vinegar, rub smooth with the yolks of hard boiled eggs, add a very little sugar, salt, mustard and cayenne pepper, beat until smooth and heat to a boil, take from the fire and pour into it a well beaten egg, whip into a smooth cream put the vessel containing this dressing in hot water while the tomatoes are being broiled over a clear fire, put the tomatoes on a hot dish and pour the dressing over them Cooked in this way, it will be a delicious accompaniment to roast chicken This is fine

STUFFED BELL PEPPER—Take one dozen bell peppers, cut in half; take out seed, take one small can of corn beef hash and a little cold beef ground up, one spoonful of butter, a few of the seeds cut up, one cup of sweet milk a tiny bit of ground onion, five or six rolled crackers, season highly with red pepper and salt to taste. Mix all together and stuff peppers, sprinkle a little of the rolled crackers over the peppers with a little melted butter poured over them, put in a pan and pour a quarter inch of water in pan around them. Cook until done.

SWISS PEPPER—Cut off the tops and remove the seed from green sweet peppers, wash and stuff with small pieces of left-over meat, chopped fine, one cup of cooked bread crumbs, two tomatoes, seasoned with chopped celery and a little extract of beef; season with salt and black pepper and lump of butter; arrange pepper in baking dish, and pour water in about half-inch deep; bake twenty minutes; serve hot

STUFFED PEPPERS—Select large bell peppers and split through center; remove the seeds and stuff with the following: Three cups of any ground cold meat, one cup of grated bread crumbs or crackers, two eggs, one small onion, one-half cup tomatoes, run through a sieve, salt and pepper, mixed together with sweet milk to right consistency. Stuff, put a little red pepper in if hot things are liked Place small bits of butter over each pepper; bake in a little water twenty minutes.

ITALIAN STUFFED TOMATOES—Cut the tops from large tomatoes and scoop out the centers; fill with left-over macaroni and cheese and the tomatoes that come out of centers, season with red pepper, dust with bread crumbs, and place lump of butter on each tomato, place in baking pan with little water and bake till tomatoes are soft; carefully lift and place each one on buttered toast; pour over a white sauce to which a hard boiled egg and a little grated cheese have been added.

DUCHESS POTATOES—Half a dozen fine potatoes mashed and rubbed through a sieve; add a little cream and the yolks of two eggs well beaten, salt and a little pepper; beat together and make into balls. Brown quickly in hot oven.

STUFFED EGG PLANTS—Boil the egg plants whole. When tender cut half in two and scoop out the pulp; mix with this pulp an equal quantity of toasted bread crumbs and one small onion, chopped fine; season this highly with butter, pepper and salt; replace in shells and sprinkle bread crumbs and small lumps of butter on top of each and place in oven to brown.

SANDWICHES

TURKEY SANDWICHES—Take bread, cut all crust off sides and put a nice layer of turkey with mayonnaise over it and cover with slice of bread

CHEESE AND PEPPER SANDWICHES—One and a half pounds of cheese, three bell peppers, slices of buttered bread; remove rind from the cheese, and remove seed and white pith from the peppers; grind peppers fine; mix thoroughly and smoothly with mayonnaise dressing, and spread between slices of bread, toast the cut side of the sandwich. Serve hot with coffee.

A NICE FILLING FOR SANDWICHES—Take one can of deviled ham, one-half bottle of Worcestershire Sauce, one-third of a pound of good butter; mix all together, keep in ice box for several days.

PECAN SANDWICHES—One pound pecan meats, one cup grated cheese; mix enough Ferndell dressing with cheese ter, then with cheese; then sprinkle thick with pecans, to make a paste; slice bread very thin, spread with but- cover with another slice of bread from which all the out- side crusts have been removed.

RAISIN SANDWICH—Grind in a meat chopper 1 lb. of seedless raisins Boil 1 cup of sugar with half cup of water till will hair. To this, add the ground raisins and stir till well mixed. Cut small slices of white bread and trim off the crust, spread one slice with peanut butter, and the other with the raisins. Place together in the usual way. One teaspoonful of butter can be added to the raisin if desired.

CLUB SANDWICHES—Arrange thin slices of cooked bacon on slices of bread, cover with slices of cold roast chicken and cover chicken with mayonnaise dressing, add two slices of iced tomato and a lettuce leaf, cover with slice of bread. The bread should be toasted a nice brown.

RUSSIAN SANDWICHES—Spread zephyrettes with thin slices of Neufchatel cheese, cover with finely chopped olives moistened with mayonnaise dressing; place zephyrette over each and press together.

SARDINE CANAPES—Spread circular pieces of bread (toasted) with sardines, from which the bones have been removed, rubbed to a paste with a small quantity of creamed butter and seasoned with Worcestershire sauce and a few grains of cayenne; place in the center of each a stuffed olive made by removing stone and filling cavity with sardine mixture. Around each, arrange a border of finely chopped whites of hard boiled eggs.

EGG AND OLIVE SANDWICHES—Chop five hard boiled eggs very fine; stone and chop fifteen large olives and mix with the egg, moisten all with three tablespoons of melted butter, season with salt and pepper and mix to a moist paste. Spread on the slices of bread and cover with mayonnaise dressing.

TOMATO AND NUT SANDWICH—Chop three medium sized tomatoes, add small green pepper chopped fine and one-half cup of chopped nuts, and a dash of mayonnaise dressing; place on lettuce leaf between thin slices of white bread, cut very thin and spread with mayonnaise.

PIMENTO SANDWICH—To one fifteen-cent box of pimentoes take a quarter of a pound of cheese, grind both cheese and pimentoes fine, drain off juice from pimentoes, mix together with a spoonful of mayonnaise, have it hot with red pepper and add a pinch of salt, slice bread thin and spread mixture on slice of bread and cover with another, press together Bread should be trimmed on edges.

OLIVE SANDWICHES—Slice bread very thin and trim off all edges. Get stuffed olives, slice round so the red will be in the middle, butter bread with the mayonnaise and cover with the sliced olives; press a thin slice of bread over the top.

A SWEET SANDWICH FILLING—Take two tablespoons of lemon juice to four of peanut butter, add one-half cup of chopped pecans and one-half cup seeded raisins, moisten with mayonnaise, and add a little sugar if you like.

DESSERTS

ORANGE PUDDING—For a family of six take one pint of sweet milk, two heaping tablespoons corn starch dissolved in a half-cup of the milk, two heaping tablespoons sugar, yolks of three eggs, beaten thoroughly, and a pinch of salt, mix all together and cook in double boiler; stir constantly, til thick and smooth, then set to cool Seed and cut into small pieces four oranges, add one cup of sugar to the oranges, mix oranges and custard together, then beat the whites of three eggs into a meringe, and put two tablespoons of sugar and a pinch of baking powder to make meringe stand up, spread over the custard, set in stove and brown.   Serve cold.

ITALIAN CREAM—Soak one-half box Knox geiatine in one cup water, dissolve over vessel of warm water, add to this one big can grated pineapple, one cup of sugar, mix all together and let come to a boil, strain through a coarse muslin cloth   When cool, but not congealed, add one pint of whipped cream, put on ice and let congeal. Serve with or without whipped cream

FIG PUDDING.—One cup seeded raisins, one cup chopped figs, one cup chopped suet, one cup sweet milk, two and one-half cups flour, one cup molasses, one teaspoon soda, one of ginger, one of cinnamon, one of nutmeg, one of salt   Add fruit, flour and spices, then pour in liquids; steam two and one-half hours.

SAUCE FOR SAME—One-half cup of butter, one cup of sugar, creamed as for cake.

BLACKBERRY JAM PUDDING—Three-fourths cup of butter, one cup of sugar, and one-half cup of flour   one

—32—

cup blackberry jam, three eggs beaten separately, three tablespoons sour cream, one teaspoon of soda, one nutmeg, bake and serve with sauce

CHOCOLATE PUDDING—One pint bread crumbs, press soaked one quart of milk; beat yolks of three eggs, and one cup of sugar with one tablespoon butter, three tablespoons chocolate grated with a little hot water; mix all together on a deep pudding dish; bake thirty minutes; flavor with vanilla. Beat the whites of the three eggs very light, add three or four tablespoons sugar and spread over pudding; brown quickly

PRUNE PUDDING WITH WHIPPED CREAM—Take one pound of prunes, wash thoroughly and cover with cold water, add three-fourths cup sugar, two tablespoons of cinnamon; let cook; when nearly done add two teaspoons of vinegar with a little flour to thicken; let cool Seed prunes and mash through collander, sweeten to taste, add seven stiffly beaten whites of eggs, flavor with vanilla and bake in a pan of water for an hour, serve cold with whipped cream sweetened and flavored.

MARSHMALLOW PUDDING—Soak two tablespoonsful of Knox Acidulated gelatine in half cup of cold water fifteen minutes; add to this one pint boiling water and half the acid Divide this, color half of it with half of the fruit tablet contained in package. Into whites of four eggs beaten very stiff, whip one and a third cups sugar, when it begins to congeal whip the pink into half of the eggs and sugar a tablespoonful at a time and pour in mold that has been dipped into cold water; now add the white gelatine flavored with a little vanilla to the other half of the eggs, add sugar, and when the pink has commenced to congeal pour the whites into it, to remove from mold, dip for an instant in hot water; serve with whipped cream.

MARSHMALLOW PUDDING NO. 2—Whites of eight eggs well beaten, two heaping tablespoons of gelatine, dissolved in two cups of boiling water; pour this slowly over the well-beaten whites, add two cups sugar, any desired flavoring; beat the whole a half hour; now take of color one-half pink (with fruit coloring in to pink part beat one cup of chopped pecans, and into white part one cup of shredded pineapples. Put into mold white part on top of pink part, let stand on ice firm, slice and serve with whipped cream.

FRUIT PUDDING—Three eggs well beaten, half cup of sugar, three tablespoons flour, package of seeded dates, cut up fine, one-fourth pound pecans, cut fine; grease pudding pan and bake in moderate oven one half-hour.

DIPLOMATIC PUDDING—One pint of milk, one-half cup of sugar, put on to boil, add beaten yolks of three eggs and stir on slow fire; add one-half box gelatine soaked in cup of milk, strain and let cool; when it begins to congeal, whip a pint of cream into the congealed part, flavor with two tablespoons of sherry wine, rum or brandy. Take layer of lady fingers and cup of raisins, put in layers and pour the custard over it. Serve with whipped cream.

ORANGE SPONGE—Cover one-half box of gelatine with half cup of water, soak ten minutes, press juice from five large oranges, add one cup of sugar, stir until dissolved. Whip one-half pint of cream, put orange juice in pan, and stand in another pan of cracked ice. Stir the gelatine over hot water until dissolved, add it to the orange juice, stir constantly; just as soon as it begins to congeal add whipped cream, stir it up together, strain and serve cold.

CHOCOLATE WHIPS—One square of chocolate, one-half cup of sugar, six eggs and a pinch of salt. Grate chocolate fine and put in pan with two tablespoons of sugar and one of boiling water; when dissolved add it to one and a half pints of sweet milk, which should be hot, in a double boiler; beat eggs and remainder of sugar together, stir constantly till it begins to thicken, add salt and set away

—34—

to cool. Season one pint of cream with two tablespoons of sugar, and one-half teaspoon of vanilla, whip cream to stiff froth. When custard is cold, half fill glasses and whipped cream upon it.

PEACH MARSHMALLOW DESSERT—Take one pound of marshmallows, pour them in a large bowl, pour over them the juice from a large can of peaches and set in ice box all night, then next day serve with whipped cream and cherries over the cream. You may use pineapple juice if preferred.

HEAVENLY DESSERT—One-half pound white grapes, cut in halves and seeded, one-half pound English walnut meats, half pound marshmallows cut in cubes, half a pound sliced pineapple, cut in cubes; pour over this one-half pint whipped cream, sweetened. Serve very cold or frozen

FROZEN PUDDING—Make a custard as for plain vanilla cream, add to the custard two tablespoons soaked gelatine. When ready to freeze add four tablespoons wine, freeze ten minutes, add one pound of candied fruit and finish freezing Serve with whipped cream.

CHARLOTTE RUSSE—Soak one-third package of gelatine in three tablespoons cold water; pour over it one-half pint of sweet milk hot, stir until gelatine is thoroughly dissolved, strain the mixture, when cool stir in one quart of whipped cream, the frothed whites of three eggs, one teaspoon of vanilla. Pour into mold lined with slices of sponge cake, and put on ice; serve with whipped cream.

STUFFED APPLES—To be served with meat. Select apples, core and bake them, fill the cavities with pecan meats and pour over them sherry wine enough to flavor; serve with whipped cream, or white of an egg; if the egg is used beat it well, add a little sugar spread over the top and place in the oven to brown.

A NICE LITTLE DESSERT—Take any nice cake batter and bake in muffin or small cake tins; when cold slice off top and remove a part of center of cake, fill opening with strawberries or chopped oranges, pineapple or any other fruit, replace the top cover with whipped cream, sweetened and flavored to taste. A few cherries or berries scattered over the top makes a very attractive dessert.

JELLY MARSHMALLOW—Use the regular jelly rule, but divide it into three parts, flavoring one part with strawberry, one with orange and one with canned blueberry juice; put each color into an individual mold and turn out on a platter. For sauce: Boil together one pint water, one-half pint granulated sugar and a pinch of salt, thicken with marshmallows and boil until clear, adding when nearly done, two tablespoons of corn starch, whip into this the beaten whites of two eggs, flavor with vanilla and one-half teaspoon of rose water; pour this around the jelly when nearly cold and grate nut meats over it.

ORANGE ROLY POLY—Make a dough like a rich biscuit dough; roll out into sheets half as long, spread this with four slices oranges, peeled and sliced and seeded, sprinkle with sugar and roll up the dough, pinching the ends together; tie the pudding in cloth, allowing the ends to swell, then drop into a pot of boiling water and boil steadily for one and a half hours. Transfer from cloth to a hot dish. Serve with hard sauce flavored with orange or lemon.

CARAMEL PUDDING—Three eggs, one pint milk, one-half cup of sugar, one teaspoon vanilla, pinch of salt. Caramelize sugar, beat eggs slightly, scald milk, add caramel to milk and eggs and bake in pudding dish.

SAUCE—One-half cup of sugar, carameled, add cup of of boiling water, cook until it forms a syrup.

SWEET POTATO AND RAISIN PUDDING—Boil and peel and mash potatoes, sweeten to taste, season with nutmeg, add a little salt, butter and as many seedless raisins as desired; mix and bake. Serve hot.

APPLE TAPIOCA PUDDING—One teacup of tapioca, one teaspoon of salt, one and one-half pints of water. Let stand several hours where it will be warm but not cook, peel six tart apples, take out the cores, fill them with sugar in which is grated a little nutmeg Put apples in pudding dish, over these pour the tapioca, first mixing it with one teaspoon of melted butter, one cup of cold milk and one-half cup of sugar Bake one hour, serve with sauce or whipped cream Any fresh fruit may be used intead of apples.

NO. 1 ENGLISH PLUM PUDDING—One-half pound stale bread crumbs, one cup of scalded milk, one-fourth pound sugar, four eggs, one-half pound of seedless raisins cut fine and floured, one-fourth pound currants, one-fourth pound finely chopped figs, two ounces finely cut citron, one-half pound suet, one-fourth cup of wine and brandy mixed, one-half of a grated nutmeg, three-fourths of a teaspoon of cinnamon, one-third teaspoon cloves, one-third teaspoon mace, one and one-half teaspoons of salt. Soak bread crumbs in milk, let stand until cool; add sugar, beaten yolks of eggs, fruit. Chop suet and cream with the hands, then add wine, brandy, spices and whites of eggs beaten stiffly. Turn into buttered mold cover and steam six hours, serve with sauce.

ORANGE JELL-O—Two packages of orange Jell-O, pour over it two and one-half pints boiling water, stir until thoroughly dissolved. Put one tablespoon of sugar in Jell-O, cut up three or four oranges in small bits without any of the stringy part or seed When Jello begins to congeal a little, put one cup of sugar over oranges, mix and pour into Jell-O, stir until well mixed, set in cool place for the night. Serve next day with whipped cream.

CHERRY DELIGHT—One-fourth pound of butter, one-fourth pound sugar, three small eggs, one-fourth pound flour, one-half teaspoon Royal Baking Powder, one tablespoon of thick cream, one-fourth teaspoon each of orange and vanilla, one-half cupful of crystalized cherries, one-third cup of bleached almonds, one-third cup of crystalized pineapple; cream the butter and gradually add the sugar until very light, then add one whole egg and beat several minutes, sift flour, measure and sift again with baking powder. Beat a little into the first mixture then add another egg, when this is beaten lightly add more flour then the cream and last egg. Drop in flavoring and beat briskly for ten minutes. Cut fruit into small pieces, roll in a little flour and stir into the batter just before pouring into tins. Bake in small muffin rings in a moderately hot oven. When ready to serve cut each one with a sharp knife in quarters or eights so that they fall open like a flower Fill the centers with whipped cream mixed with a few cut marshmallows, a little powdered sugar, and a few cherries to flavor.

APPLE DESSERT—Take as many apples as needed, peel and core, put sugar enough to sweeten and cover with water sufficient to boil until done. Make a boiled custard in double boiler. After apples are done, (don't break them) pour the custard over apples and take whites of eggs and make meringe and put over the whole, sprinkle with nutmeg and brown slightly. Serve cold

CUSTARD PUFFS—Boil one cup hot water, half cup of butter While boiling stir in one cup of sifted flour, remove from fire and stir to a smooth paste When cool add three unbeaten eggs and stir five minutes, bake in slow oven, just drop dabs off spoon in pan to make puffs.

CUSTARD FILLING—One pint milk, three eggs, half cup of sugar, two tablespoons of corn starch, pinch of salt, butter size of an egg, teaspoon vanilla, cream, butter and sugar and cook in double boiler until thick and creamy, then cut off top of puff and fill with the custard.

LEMON PIGS—Take a whole lemon, leave the little stub end for a nose, paint underneath with ink for a mouth, dot eyes with ink and cut little square places on the sides for ears, and turn the peeling back, cut off the rounding side and scoop out all of the lemon. Break two tooth picks and put under lemon for pigs legs, put a piece of grape vine on the back for the tail, fill up through the hole on the side with chicken salad, with mayonnaise on top Take lettuce and chop fine, put pig on plate and mound lettuce up to his mouth in front and let shredded lettuce go all way round the pig. You will find this a very attractive dish to serve for a child's party.

A PRETTY SHERBERT FOR AN ENTERTAINMENT— Color your sherbert green with fruit coloring and serve in tall sherbert glasses; have a fancy plate with paper lace doily on it and serve glasses of sherbert on plate. Serve with white whipped cream mounted on top of sherbet and lay a white rose with green leaves on one side of plate and green and white cake on the other side.

WHITE CARAMEL FILLING OR CREAM FILLING— Two cups sugar, one cup butter, one cup cream; put in double boiler until sugar is dissolved; let boil five minutes, lift up and let boil a little more

CORN PUDDING—To one can of corn add a generous cup of sweet milk, two eggs well beaten, one teaspoon of sugar, salt and pepper to taste, two tablespoons of melted butter; let cook in slow oven

ALMOND BISQUE—Two pints of sweet milk, one-half pint shelled almonds, one tablespoon flour, one of butter Begin by making a white sauce of your butter and milk Blanch your almonds by pouring hot water over them and taking skin off and while hot grind and run in hot oven to brown, then add the sauce and cook three or four minutes, season with salt and pepper to taste This serves fifteen bouillon cups two-thirds full. One spoon of whipped cream dropped in each cup with a little ground almonds sprinkled over each cup Serve hot.

CINNAMON APPLES—Six medium sized apples peeled

and cored, two cupfuls of sugar, two bananas, one cupful of water, one-half cup of cinnamon candy drops. Make a syrup, when boiling put in apples stuffed with bananas or two or three cinnamon drops, then put into syrup, sprinkle rest of candy over apples This makes a lovely pink color and gives a delightful flavor. Put in dish and serve cold with meat.

FRUIT GELATINE—Half dozen oranges, fifteen-cent bottle maraschino cherries with juice, half cup sugar one cup cold water, one enevelope gelatine, soak gelatine first in cold water then in hot, to which sugar has been added Set away to cool and let congeal. Serve with whipped cream

FISH PUDDING—Two pounds fish, two eggs, grated onions to taste Cook fish until tender in a little water to which a little salt has been added. When done remove bones and mash. To the fish add white sauce-onion and eggs beaten together until very light Grease mold, put in fish mixture and set in pan of hot water. Allow to steam for forty minutes keeping water just below boiling point. Before putting into oven cover pudding with oiled paper Garnish with sliced lemon and parsley.

PIES

OLD FASHIONED GREEN APPLE PIES—Take one or two dozen apples, peel and cut up, put on top of stove with a little water in pan or kettle, let boil till they mash up, strain through a sifter, sweeten to taste, and put a good sized lump of butter in and flavor with nutmeg. Bake between two rich crusts

APPLE FLOAT—Fix apples just like above, strain and sweeten to taste, let get cold, beat whites of three eggs, beat into the apples until light, flavor with nutmeg. Serve cold with whipped cream, with a little sugar in it.

STRAWBERRY SHORT CAKE—Make a rich pie crust, roll very thin and bake on flat tin; take fresh berries, wash and pick; put sugar over them and mash up; when ready to serve, take knife and spread strawberries over a layer of pie crust and so on until you fix a stack four or five layers high. Make a sauce as follows: Take two cups of sugar, one heaping tablespoon of butter, two spoons of sifted flour, pour juice out of pan into sauce, slice short cake, and serve with plenty sauce poured over it.

APPLE ROLL—Cut up apples with core out, make rich pie crust, lay it half across pan with top turned back, put a good deal of sugar over apples, also butter and sprinkle nutmeg or cinnamon over the whole. Turn top back over apples and sprinkle sugar over the top with small lumps of butter and cinnamon or nutmeg. Put pan half full of water with a cup of sugar in it and let cook slowly until nicely browned The water and sugar make the sauce.

SWEET POTATO CUSTARD—Take several potatoes, according to the number to eat, boil them done and peel;

mix with two cups sweet milk, rub through a sifter and sweeten to taste, beat six eggs separately, put in the yolks and sugar and tablespoon of butter; lastly add the whites well beaten, stir them up in mixture, make custard about as thick as batter cakes, so if necessary add more milk; add one pinch of salt and flavor with lemon; bake in rich pie crust.

PUMPKIN PIE NO. 1—Two each part of condensed pumpkin, add four well beaten eggs, one-half teaspoon of salt, one-half cup of molasses, and one scant quart of milk, add sugar to taste and then, gradually add any desired amount of spices, cinnamon and ginger and a little nutmeg. Line deep pie dishes with pastry, fill the prepared pumpkin and bake in a moderate oven. Serve very cold. Just before serving cover top of pie with stiffly whipped cream and dot cream with walnuts or raisins.

PUMPKIN PIE NO. 2—Three cups pumpkin or kershaw, yolks of four eggs, two cups of sugar, one teaspoon of cinnamon and one of ginger, one pint of sweet milk; use whites of four eggs for meringue; make two pies.

BUTTERMILK PIE—For four pies, six eggs, four cups of sugar, one cup butter, five tablespoons corn starch, two cups buttermilk; season with nutmeg and vanilla.

BUTTERMILK CUSTARD NO. 2—This is fine. One cup of buttermilk, one cup raisins, four yolks of eggs, butter size of an egg, two large tablespoonsful of flour, one teaspoon of cinnamon, one of cloves and one of nutmeg. Mix all together; put in a raw crust and bake; take the four whites and four tablespoons of sugar and tiny bit of Royal Baking Powder, beat stiffly and spread over the pies as meringue.

CREAM PIE—Yolk of three eggs, one cup sugar, two tablespoons flour, two and a half cups of milk, pinch of salt; cook in a double boiler, flavor with vanilla. Take whites and make a meringue.

PIE CRUST—Three cups of flour, one cup of lard, one level teaspoonful of salt, rub the lard thoroughly through the flour, then add a half cup of ice water and mix. Don't put baking powder in pie crust.

JELLY PIE—One-half cup of butter, two of sugar, creamed together, four eggs and one cup of acid jelly; bake in lower crust in pie pans.

MOLASSES PIE No. 1—One cup of molasses, half cup of sugar, two eggs and lump of butter size of walnut, two tablespoons of sifted flour.

MOLASSES PIE No. 2—Three eggs, one cup of sugar, two tablespoons flour in sugar, one cup molasses and teaspoon of melted butter.

LEMON PIE NO 1—Five eggs beaten light, two cups of sugar, juice of two lemons and rind of one; one tablespoon of flour mixed with a little water, and one tablespoon of butter; mix all together and pour in pans lined with crusts and bake.

LEMON PIE NO. 2—This is fine   Take eight eggs, reserve whites of four, take yolks and remaining whites and beat with two cups of sugar, two tablespoons flour mixed with sugar dry, a large tablespoon of butter, grated rind and juice of two lemons, one-half cup of water; this makes two pies.   Beat whites stiff and add sugar for meringue

TEXAS PECAN PIE—One cup of sugar, one of sweet milk, one-half cup of pecan kernels chopped fine, three eggs, one tablespoon flour.   When cooked, spread the whites of two eggs well beaten with two tablespoons of sugar on top, brown and sprinkle a few of the chopped kernels over it.

LEMON PIE NO. 3—Juice and grated rind of one lemon, one cup of sugar, one of water, one tablespoon of flour, yolks of two eggs well beaten; mix all together, and cook in basin over water until thick, then pour into the baked crusts.   Whip the whites of two eggs to a stiff froth with two tablespoonsful of sugar; pour on top of pie and set in hot oven.

JELLY CUSTARD NO. 3—Yolks of four eggs, one cup sugar, butter the size of an egg, four tablespoons sweet milk, four tablespoons jelly, and last the whites of the eggs, and about two tablespoons of sifted flour.

CHOCOLATE PIE—Make and bake one crust, mix one cup of grated chocolate with one cup of water, butter size of an egg, one cup of sugar, one tablespoon of vanilla, two tablespoons of corn starch and two eggs well beaten; cook until thick, stirring constantly; pour in crust and ice top and put in oven to brown; this makes one pie.

COCOANUT PIE—One cup sugar, three eggs, two cups milk. Mix one heaping teacup cocoanut with eggs and sugar, beat whites of two eggs to froth, stirring in two tablespoons of sugar; make meringue, put over pie and bake light brown. One tablespoon of corn starch mixed in custard will improve it. Flavor with vanilla.

CHEESE PIE—Yolks of three eggs and whites of one, three tablespoons melted butter, one cup of sugar, three table-spoons sweet milk, one tablespoon flour, flavor with va-nilla or lemon. Bake with under crust to nice brown. Take two remaining whites and two tablespoons sugar, beat till stiff; place on pie and brown slightly.

BANANA PIE—Yolks of three eggs, tablespoon sugar and a pinch of salt, tablespoon flour, one cup of sweet milk, one teaspoon of vanilla; cook until thick in double boiler, then pour into crust already baked; slice thin one banana over custard. Beat whites of eggs with four tablespoons su-gar and pour over pie. Return to oven and brown.

MOCK CHERRY PIE—One cup of chopped cranberries, one of chopped raisins, half cup of water, two tablespoons flour, one cup sugar, two tablespoons butter, teaspoon of vanilla. Bake between two crusts.

PINEAPPLE PIE—One small can of grated pineapple with

most of the juice drained off, the same measure of sugar, half as much butter, one cup of cream, five eggs, beat butter to a creamy froth, add sugar and yellows of eggs, beat until very light, add the cream and pineapple and whites of eggs; beat to a stiff froth.   Bake with an under crust.

PECAN AND RAISIN PIE—Two cups sweet milk, two eggs, two tablespoons flour, one pinch salt, one cup sugar one cup chopped pecans, one cup chopped raisins, one teaspoon of vanilla.   Make custard in double boiler and put in a baked crust.   Bake with a meringue

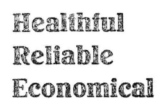
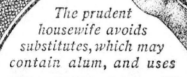

CAKES

FRUIT CAKE NO. 1—Twelve eggs beaten sepaitely, one pound of butter, one of sugar, one of sifted flour, three pounds of raisins, two pounds currants, one pound of citron, two pounds of almonds (if desired), one tablespoonful each of ground spice, cloves and cinnamon; one-half pint of sherry wine, one-half pint of whiskey. Dredge fruit in flour, if baked in one pan the cake requires seven hours, if in two cakes, three hours for baking.

FRUIT CAKE NO 2—Seven eggs, one cup butter, one of sugar, one-half cup of molasses, one-half teaspoon of soda, one-half pound of citron, one of currants, one of almonds, cut fine, one tablespoon of cinnamon, one-half teaspoon of cloves, one quart sifted flour, five drops of essence of almond. Directions for mixing: Beat eggs separately, wash and dry currants the day before, mix butter, sugar and yolks together, then add molasses, then fruit, then flour, then whites of eggs; mix all fruit together, and flour and spice it before putting into batter   Cook three hours in a moderate oven

FRUIT CAKE NO. 3—One pound of white sugar, one of flour, three-quarters pound butter, whites of sixteen eggs, two cocoanuts, grated, one-half pound of almonds, bleach-ed and chopped fine, two pounds of citron, sliced thin, one teaspoon of soda, two of cream of tartar, dissolved in cream.

FINE WHITE CAKE—One cup sweet milk or water, whites of eight eggs, two cups sugar, three and a half cups sifted flour, one-half pound white butter, two round teaspoons of Royal Baking Powder, cream, butter and sugar well, sift baking powder and mix thoroughly in flour, whip the eggs to a light but not hard froth, flavor with two teaspoons of lemon extract, or any preferred flavoring, bake in moderate oven.

SPLENDID YELLOW CAKE—Yellows of eight eggs, three-fourths cup of butter, one cup of sugar, two cups sifted flour, one-half cup of sweet milk, one heaping teaspoon of Royal Baking Powder—flavor to suit the taste and bake.

POUND CAKE—Five eggs, one cup butter, two cups sugar, four cups of flour, one cup of sweet milk, two teaspoons Royal Baking Powder; mix and bake in moderate oven after flavoring with two teaspoons of vanilla extract.

WHITE CAKE—Whites of nine eggs, two cups sugar, one cup of sweet milk, one scant cup of butter, four cups of sifted flour, two teaspoons cream tartar, one teaspoon soda, pinch of salt.

WHITE LOAF CAKE—Whites of 10 eggs, 4 scant cups of flour, 2 cups sugar, 2 scant teaspoons of Royal Baking Powder, 1 cup of butter, 1 cup milk.

WHITE CAKE—Whites of six eggs, two cups sugar, three and one-half cups flour, three-fourths cup of milk, one cup of butter, two level teaspoons Royal Baking Powder. Cream butter and sugar well together, then add flour and milk alternately and lastly beaten whites, flavor with vanilla or lemon flavoring. Bake in layers and spread with the following: Three cups sugar, one of water; boil till it threads, and pour into beaten whites of three eggs.

CARAMEL CAKE—Three and a half cups of flour, two cups of sugar, one cup of butter, one cup sweet milk, three teaspoons Royal Baking Powder, six eggs beaten well, separately; mix together and bake in layers. Following is filling for same: Two cups sugar, wet soft with sweet milk, one heaping teaspoon of butter, cook until it strings from spoon, beat or grind up one cup of nut meats, add to cooked sugar, beat up and flavor to taste with vanilla and spread between layers while hot.

PRINCE OF WALES CAKE—Whites of eight eggs, two level cups of sugar, one cup of butter, one of sweet milk, four cups flour, two heaping teaspoons of Royal Baking Powder, mix cream, butter and sugar together first, then add two cups of flour with the baking powder sifted into it, then the cup of milk, then the other two cups of flour, then the whites beaten stiff; bake half of the batter in two white layers, take the other half and put one heaping teaspoonful of spice, one of cinnamon in it, one-half package of seeded raisins, cut fine and roll in flour and mix with batter and bake in two layers. Make an icing and when nearly done, drop one-half pound of marshmallows into it and let melt; beat whites of two eggs stiff and beat into the boiled syrup and marshmallows, ice each layer and put together with one of the white and one of the dark cakes alternately.

ORANGE CAKE—Take whites of eight eggs, beaten stiff, two level cups of sugar, one of butter, four cups of flour, one cup of milk, two heaping teaspoons of Royal Baking Powder, flavor with lemon extract

FILLING FOR SAME—Yolks of three eggs, beat thoroughly, juice of two or three oranges, sweeten to taste, two tablespoons of sifted flour, mix all together and cook in double boiler, stir constantly till thick and smooth, ice the layers separately and let cool and harden, then put filling between layers.

GOOD CAKE—To make the white layers use the whites of six eggs, one-half cup of butter, two and one-half cups of sugar, three cups of flour, two teaspoons of Royal Baking Powder, one scant teacup of milk, flavor to taste For the dark layers, take the yolks of six eggs, one-half cup of butter, two cups sugar, three cups flour, scant cup of sweet milk, two teaspoons of Royal Baking Powder, one and a half blocks of chocolate grated, flavor with vanilla. Put together alternately after icing Use following filling: One cup of sugar, boiled with one-half cup water till it will rope, add to this one cup seeded and ground raisins.

—49—

WHITE CAKE—Whites of six eggs, two cups of sugar, three cups flour, one cup of sweet milk, one cup of butter, two teaspoons Royal Baking Powder, one teaspoon lemon extract.

GOOD DINNER CAKE—Two eggs, one cup of sugar, two of flour, one tablespoon of butter, one-half cup of sweet milk, two teaspoons Royal Baking Powder.

TEA CAKES—One cup of butter, one of sweet milk, five cups flour, three eggs, beaten separately, two tablespoons Royal Baking Powder. Drop about two tablespoons in a place on a buttered tin and bake in hot oven.

TEA CAKES NO. 2—Eight tablespoonsful of sugar, six tablespoons melted butter, four tablespoons sweet milk, two eggs, one heaping teaspoon Royal Baking Powder, one tablespoon lemon or vanilla flavoring, flour sufficient to roll; roll very thin and dip in granulated sugar before baking. Delicious.

TEA CAKES NO. 3—Three cups sugar, two of lard, three eggs, ten cents worth of oil of lemen; get five cents worth of baker's amonia, but use only one-third at a time and dissolve it in a pint of sweet milk, mix, add together and work in flour enough to roll thin and cut out in fancy shapes and bake on buttered tins.

SOFT GINGER CAKE—Four eggs, one-half cup of brown sugar, one of butter, four cups flour, one cup of molasses, one spoon of soda, one cup butter milk, one tablespoon of ginger. Serve with sauce.

SILVER CAKE—Whites of sixteen eggs, one cup butter, four cups sugar, six cups flour, one and a half cups milk, two teaspoons Royal Baking Powder; flavor with lemon or rose.

WHITE CARAMEL CAKE—Two and one-half cups sugar, one cup butter, well creamed, one and half cups sweet milk, four and one-half cups sifted flour, whites of nine eggs, beaten to a stiff froth, two teaspoons of Royal Baking Powder, one teaspoon of flavoring; bake in layers.

CUP CAKE—Four eggs, three cups sifted flour, two cups sugar, one cup sweet milk, one cup butter, two teaspoons Royal Baking Powder; flavored as desired.

BOSTON TEA CAKES—Two cups flour, one cup of milk, one and one half cups sugar, two eggs, three teaspoons Royal Baking Powder, one tablespoon melted butter.

SOFT GINGER BREAD—One half cup sugar, one cup molasses, one-half cup of butter, one teaspoon each of ginger and cloves, one teaspoon soda dissolved in cup of boiling water, two and half cups flour, lastly two well beaten eggs.

INDIAN CAKE—One-half cup of butter, one and half cups sugar, whites of six eggs, one cup sweet milk, two and one-half cups flour, two teaspoons Royal Baking Powder; bake in three layers

FILLING FOR SAME—One cup sugar, four tablespoons water, boiled together till clear, stir it into the beaten white of one egg, add one-half cup seeded raisins, one-half cup nuts, both chopped fine.

BLACKBERRY JAM CAKE—Two cups sugar, four cups flour, one cup butter, one cup of jam, one cup of buttermilk, one cup of grapes or raisins, three eggs, beaten separately, one small nutmeg grated, one teaspoon cinnamon, and last add 2 teaspoons of soda, dissolved in little warm water, beat well and bake in layers.

JAM CAKE NO. 2—Four eggs, one and a half cups sugar, one cup butter, four tablespoons sour cream or buttermilk, one teaspoon soda, one of spice, cloves and cinnamon, one grated nutmeg and one-half cup of jam, mix rather thick with flour, bake in layers and put together with icing and pecans.

PORK CAKE—One cup raw salt pork, chopped fine, one cup of sugar, one raisins, one of currants, one of molasses, one of sweet milk, one egg, one teaspoon of soda, one of cloves, one of cinnamon; stir in enough flour to make a little thicker than common cake.

MARBLE CAKE (White Part)—Whites of seven eggs three cups white sugar, one cup butter, one cup of sweet milk, one teaspoon soda, two teaspoons cream tartar, four and one-half cups flour, flavor with lemon.

DARK PART—Yolks of seven eggs, one cup each brown sugar, molasses, butter and sweet milk, one teaspoon soda, two of cream of tartar, five cups flour sifted; one dessert spoon each of cinnamon, cloves and spice, two grated nutmegs.

NEVER FAIL WHITE CAKE—Cream together one cup of butter and two of sugar, add the whites of four eggs that have been well beaten, one-half cup each of milk and water, three cups of flour, into which has been sifted two level teaspoons of Royal Baking Powder.

RIBBON CAKE (White Part)—Take whites of eight eggs well beaten, two level cups sugar, one cup of butter; cream butter and sugar together and add two level cups sifted flour, two heaping teaspoons Royal Baking Powder, put into sugar and butter, then pour one cup sweet milk into mixture, then two more level cups flour, then the whites of eggs; flavor with lemon; beat well; bake two layers white, then take the other half of batter, put enough fruit coloring to make a good pink, chop one cup of pecan nuts, roll in flour and put in pink batter, and bake in two layers, ice each layer, then take a can of grated pineapple, squeeze out the juice and put the layers together, alternating the white and pink with pineapple between each layer.

SNOW CAKE—Sift together four times, one and one-half cups of flour, one cup sugar, one heaping teaspoon Royal Baking Powder, into the same cup put whites of two eggs, butter the size of an egg, and fill cup with sweet milk, add this to sifted ingredients and beat hard for two minutes. Bake in layers.

SOFT GINGER CAKE—Two eggs well beaten, one cup molasses, one buttermilk, one sugar, one-half cup butter, four cups flour, one tablespoon soda; cream sugar and butter together; add one tablespoon each, ginger, cloves and spice.

GINGER BREAD—Take one-half cup of butter, one-half cup sugar, one-half cup molasses, one-half cup sour milk, two eggs, one-half teaspoon soda, one-half teaspoon each of ginger and cinnamon, two cups flour, one cup seeded raisins, mix well, this bread keeps soft many days and its flavor improves with age.

JAPANESE CAKE—Two cups sugar, one cup butter, one cup sweet milk, four eggs, one teaspoon Royal Baking Powder, four cups flour. After mixing this in usual way divide batter, taking one-third; add one cup of chopped nuts; to the other two-thirds, add one-half pound seeded raisins, chopped fine, one-half teaspoon each of cloves, cinnamon and allspice. Bake in three layers with nut layer in center. Make filling as follows: One small cocoanut, two cups sugar, one cup hot water, rind and juice of two lemons, one tablespoon of corn starch; cook to a thick cream.

SPICE CAKE—One and one-fourth cups of butter, two and a half cups sugar, five cups flour, one cup sour milk, five eggs, one teaspoon soda, one teaspoon each of cloves, spice, cinnamon and nutmeg, one-half cup chocolate.

WHITE PERFECTION CAKE—Whites of ten eggs, one cup butter, three cups sugar, five cups flour, two teaspoons Royal Baking Powder; flavor with lemon or flavor to taste.

ANGEL FOOD CAKE—Whites of eleven eggs, one and a half cups sugar, one flour, one level teaspoon cream of tartar, one teaspoon vanilla; sift flour five times, measuring before sifting; sift sugar once; break eggs into a bowl; beat till stiff but not hard, then add cream of tartar and beat for five minutes, then add sugar, beating all the time, then fold in flour and lastly vanilla, bake in pan that has not been greased.

FRUIT CAKE—One pound sugar, one of butter, one of flour, twelve eggs, three pounds seedless raisins, one pound citron, two pounds currants, one of pecans, one of walnuts, one of almonds, two teaspoons each of spice, cinnamon and nutmeg, one cup of brandy; flour fruits well and mix in the usual way.

OLD FASHIONED GOLD AND SILVER CAKE (Silver)— Whites of eight eggs, two cups sugar, one cup butter, one cup sweet milk, three cups flour, one heaping teaspoon Royal Baking Powder; flavor with lemon to taste. Bake in four layers.

GOLD—Yolk eight eggs, three-quarters cup of butter, one-half cup sweet milk, one cup sugar, one and a half cups flour, two level teaspoons of Royal Baking Powder, vanilla to taste. Bake in three layers.

MARSHMALLOW FILLING—One cup of sugar, one-half cup water, whites of two eggs, well beaten, ten cent box marshmallows; cook sugar and water till it ropes; pour into the beaten whites, beaitng all the time, add marshmallows and beat till they are thoroughly dissolved.

CARAMEL FILLING—Four cups brown sugar, two cups milk, one-half cup of butter, brown sugar in kettle, then add milk and dissolve well, then butter and cook until thick as candy and beat well. Spread between layers of cake.

CHOCOLATE ICING—Three cups sugar, one cup milk, yellow of two eggs, one tablespoon of butter, one-half cake Baker's Chocolate; flavor with vanilla. Cook as caramel filling.

BOILED ICING—Two cups sugar, one cup water; cook till

it hardens in cold water; have the whites of two eggs well beaten, and when the syrup is done add to eggs and beat constantly, adding juice of half lemon.

MAPLE FILLING FOR CAKE—Three-fourths cup of maple sugar, two tablespoons butter; cook until it threads; pour gradually into stiffly beaten whites of two eggs, beat it until smooth.

TRIED AND TESTED FRUIT CAKE—One pound butter, one of sugar, one dozen eggs beaten separately, one pound citron cut fine, two pounds currants, two pounds raisins, one pound sifted flour, two teaspoons each of cinnamon, nutmeg, cloves and spice. Two cups chopped pecans, or one of pecans and one of almonds blanched and chopped fine. After all are cut fine dredge in flour, (flour that has already been weighed). Three-fourths pint of whiskey or sweet milk. Fifteen cents worth of cherries and one-half pound of pineapple. If you use pineapple and cherries, use only one-half pound of citron, one teaspoon of Royal Baking Powder. Cook about six hours if one cake is to be made If to be divided into two cakes only three and one-half hours will be required for cooking

WHITE FRUIT CAKE—The whites of one dozen eggs, one pound sifted flour, one cup of butter, one pound of sugar, two heaping teaspoons of Royal Baking Powder, one-half pound of citron chopped fine, one teacup of chopped almonds, one-half pound or less of chopped crystalized pineapple, two cups grated cocoanut, one cup of sweet milk, and if too stiff add more milk. To mix, cream sugar and butter, then part of the flour, mix fruit and nuts chopped fine and cocoanut, rub them in the other flour and then put all together. Sift Royal Baking Powder in the first flour you use. Add milk, then whites of eggs beaten stiffly. Flavor with lemon.

ORNAMENTAL FROSTING—Two cups sugar, one cup water, whites three eggs, one-fourth teaspoon tartaric acid, boil sugar and water until syrup forms a thread when dropped from the spoon. Pour syrup gradually on beaten whites of eggs beating constantly, then add acid and continue beating; when stiff enough to spread put a thin coating over the cake. Beat remaining frosting until cold and stiff enough to keep in shape after being forced through a pastry tube. After first coating on the cake has hardened cover with a thicker layer and crease for cutting. If frosting is too stiff to spread smoothly thin with a few drops of water. With a pastry bag and a variety of tubes cake may be ornamented as desired.

PINK AND WHITE CAKES—The whites of six eggs, three cups of flour, one and three-quarter cups of sugar, one cup of milk, one light cup of butter, three level teaspoons of Royal Baking Powder. Flavor to taste. Color one half pink and bake in layers and put together with any desired filling.

LADY BALTIMORE CAKE—Make a six-egg white cake. Flavor with rose water, with white icing, put with following filling: One cup of raisins, cut in pieces, one cup of pecans or walnuts, cut half a cup of figs if liked. Mix this with icing and put between layers. Ice top plain and put fruit on top cake. Use the raisins and whole nuts in half and figs in strips.

THE GRAPE JUICE CAKE—One cup butter, two cups of sugar, six eggs (both whites and yolks), one cup sweet milk, three-quarters cup of flour, half cup grape juice. Four level teaspoons of Royal Baking Powder, two teaspoons cinnamon, one heaping tablespoon cocoa, one cup blackberry jam. Cream butter and add one-half the sugar, beating very light. Beat yolks and other half the sugar, sift flour twice, flour and baking powder together, all this in turn with milk and beaten egg whites to butter, eggs and sugar mixture. Mix spices and cocoa to grape juice and add to batter. Last gently stir in jam.

A COTTOLENE CAKE—Cream one-half cup of cottolene add one cup sugar and mix together one-half cup milk and two cups pastry flour in which two teaspoons of Royal Baking Powder and a pinch of salt have been well sifted. Beat well, add well beaten yolks and whites of three eggs. Separately bake in two layers   Use any kind of filling.

WHITE ORANGE CAKE—One cup butter, two cups sugar, three cups flour, whites of five eggs, two teaspoons of Royal Baking Powder, three-quarters cup of milk, and the juice of one orange, strain if very juicy   Use a little less milk as you want about one small cup of all   Add also a teaspoon of extract of orange juice to batter   Cook in two layers and put together with orange icing made by pulverizing sugar with orange juice and extract of oranges   If oranges are not acid add a little lemon juice. This is fine.

AN IRISH POTATO CAKE—Three eggs, one cup butter, two cups sugar, three cups flour, one-half cup of sweet milk, one-half cup of grated chocolate, one cup boiled Irish potatoes mashed, one cup pecans mashed and rolled in flour, two teaspoons of Royal Baking Powder, one teaspoon spice, one spoon cloves, one spoon cinnamon, cream butter and sugar, then add chocolate   Beat in eggs, then potatoes, milk, flour, pecans and spices.

SAUCES

WINE SAUCE—Beat together until light one cup sugar, (powdered) with one egg and the yolk of a second; add in a wine glass of wine, heated very hot.

MAPLE SAUCE—An agreeable sauce with a steam pudding is made by dissolving a half pint of maple sugar in a cup of water; add half cup of butter, mixed with one table-spoon of flour, flavor to taste

HARD SAUCE—Beat together one cup of sugar and half cup of butter, flavor to taste, form into a pyramid and shape to suit the fancy.

BROWN SAUCE FOR CAKE OR PUDDING—Mix half cup of brown sugar with half the quantity of butter; add pint of hot water and a little vinegar with such flavoring as may be desired; use a tablespoonful of flour, moistened with milk and boil   Should be served hot.

TOMATO SAUCE—Take four medium sized tomatoes, or one small can and one small onion, cut the tomatoes up and cook with onions until the juice is out of the toma-toes, strain into another sauce pan, put it on stove; add a tablespoon of flour, and butter the size of an egg. Rub the flour into butter, season with salt and pepper; pour this into a platter and lay slices of tongue or other suit-able meats on it.

CHICKEN SALAD DRESSING—Four yolks of eggs, beat-en, one cup of vinegar, butter size of an egg, two table-spoons of mustard, mixed with a little vinegar, one table-spoon of sugar, cook, salt afterwards, add one-half cup of whipped cream just before using.

SAUCE TO BE EATEN ON ICE COLD TOMATOES—One egg beaten well, one teaspoon of sugar, half teaspoon celery seed ground, one level teaspoon salt, one-fourth teaspoon black pepper, two teaspoons mustard, one cup vinegar; cook till it thickens This sauce keeps well.

DELMONICO SALAD DRESSING—One hard boiled egg, chopped fine, one teaspoon tomato catsup, one of Worcestershire sauce, two tablespoons of olive oil, one-fourth teaspoon of chopped green peppers, a dash of cayenne pepper and salt to taste, two tablespoons of vinegar; mix and serve cold on lettuce, tomato or other vegetables. A tiny pinch of sugar may improve it.

WHITE SAUCE—Take two cups of sweet milk and one heaping tablespoon of butter, two tablespoons sifted flour, mixed in a little cold milk and stirred into the other milk; cook until a little thick and creamy; season with salt and pepper to taste.

MAYONNAISE DRESSING (Made With Olive Oil)—Take yolks of two eggs without a particle of the whites, beat them thoroughly, then stir in your olive oil; let run very slowly and stir constantly till it begins to get thick; add a little lemon juice and more oil and so on, until you get as much made as you want, then stir in a plentiful supply of salt and red pepper, if it should become curdled and oily again, break another yellow and stir in all of the curdled mixture slowly like you did from the first.

SOUR SAUCE FOR FISH AND MEAT—Take half a dozen large green peppers, ground fine, add three large onions chopped fine, mix together, then make a mixture of five gills of vinegar, sweeten to taste, add salt and pepper, just a little catsup; beat this into the pepper and onions, put on stove and boil until soft. A little celery seed may be added if the flavor is desired; when cool set away till wanted, and I assure you this is fine.

A FRENCH SAUCE FOR ASPARAGUS—Thick white

sauce poured over yolks of eggs, beaten well while boiling hot; pour very slowly; add juice of one lemon; serve cold.

DRESSING FOR FISH—Six hard boiled eggs, one-quarter pint of vinegar, salt, pepper and celery seed to taste Mash the yolks of the eggs and mix with vinegar, butter the size of an egg; chop the whites into small pieces and set all on stove to boil thick; if vinegar is too strong, add water.

A WHITE MAYONNAISE—One-half cup corn starch, one-half cup cold water, one cup boiling water. Dissolve corn starch in cold water, add this to boiling water while on stove. Stir until thick, take from fire and add at once the yolks of two eggs beaten When cool add one cup of oil, juice of two lemons and salt and cayenne pepper.

SALADS

TOMATO JELLY SALAD—To one can of tomatoes, add one-third as much water as there are tomatoes, boil a few minutes and rub through a collander, using the tomato juice; add one-quarter box of Knox's gelatine, dissolved in a cup of cold water, then melted over hot water; season with salt, pepper and tobasco sauce (make pretty hot) one teaspoonful of vinegar; mix all together; put in molds and allow to harden; serve on lettuce leaves with a spoonful of mayonnaise on top of each.

WALDORF SALAD—Take six apples, peel and cut fine; cut ten cents worth of celery fine; half cup of pecan meats, and make the following dressing; let it get cold and mix all with the salad.

DRESSING FOR WALDORF SALAD—Take two eggs and beat together, add one cup of sweet milk, half cup of vinegar, one tablespoon of butter, a good pinch of salt, a heaping tablespoon of sugar, two tablespoons of sifted flour; mix all together and let boil till thick; stir constantly; it will at first look curdled and will lump, but that won't hurt, keep stirring until the mixture gets smooth and thick, let cool before putting over mixture

FRUIT SALAD—For a family of six, take four oranges, three apples, ten cents worth of celery, a small can of sliced pineapple, half cup of pecans, one banana, (not necessary but good) Cut all up fine. Be careful not get the seed of the oranges in the fruit, as it will make it bitter; mix all together and put one tablespoonful of sugar, if not sweet enough to suit, add more sugar; serve on lettuce leaves with whipped cream.

GRAPE FRUIT SALAD—Take pulp of three grape fruits, one pound of white grapes, half cup of pecans, one fifteen-cent can of pineapple, all cut fine together, sweeten to taste; serve on lettuce leaves with mayonnaise dressing on the grape fruit if preferred.

PEAR SALAD—Take one can of pears, put one slice on lettuce leaf on saucer, chop a little celery, sprinkle a little chopped pecans over every slice and serve with mayonnaise dressing.

CHICKEN SALAD—Take one chicken; dress and leave it whole; put in a pot of water and boil till tender; when thoroughly tender, cut up into small pieces; cut fifteen cents worth of celery, one cup of pecans into small bits, put one cup of liquor over mixture. Take three hard boiled eggs, mash the yolks up with two spoons of vinegar, and stir into mixture; salt to taste; cut the whites up into mixture; rub in plenty of red and bleck pepper; make a mayonnaise dressing and stir into the mixture.

TOMATO JELLY SALAD NO. 2—Strain a can of tomatoes and season well, especially with salt; heat to boiling and add half box of gelatine, dissolve in hot water; pour into molds and when firm, serve on lettuce leaves.

CHESSE SALAD—Half pound American cheese, grated, one pint of whipped cream, salt and pepper to taste, one tablespoonful of powdered gelatine, four tablespoons boiling water; dissolve the gelatine in hot water; strain and add cheese and whipped cream, and seasoning of salt and pepper, pour into wet mold and allow it to become firm; turn out; cut in slices, place each slice on lettuce leaves and serve with boiled dressing or mayonnaise. This will serve twelve people.

BANANA SALAD—Place a lettuce leaf on as many saucers as you wish to serve guests; on each lettuce leaf, put two thin slices of banana; cut up fine, celery and pecan meats over each, sprinkle with grated cheese and serve with a mayonnaise dressing.

STUFFED TOMATO SALAD—Take as many tomatoes as you have people to serve, slice off stem and remove pulp and seed; chop one-half cup of pecan meats, grind up three bell peppers, ten cents worth of celery chopped fine, season with salt and pepper to taste (red pepper), mix with tomato pulp and mayonnaise dressing, drain the juice from the mixture, after removing from the ice box or refrigerator fill the tomato hulls with mixture and serve at once on lettuce leaves, cover with mayonnaise. This is fine

SHRIMP SALAD—Two cans of shrimps, drain, let stand in cold water till ready for use; break in halves. Take one can of tomatoes, drain thoroughly, two cups celery chopped fine, one cup cracker crumbs, four tablespoons vinegar, two of water, one of butter, one-half teaspoon salt, one-eighth teaspoon cayenne pepper, half teaspoon sugar, piece of onion, let come to a boil, take out onion when cool, add teaspoon of Worcestershire, a little lemon juice and pour over shrimp

PERFECTION SALAD—Small quantity of shredded cabbage, one can of pimento, ground, one can of tomato juice with the pulp strained out, season with salt, lemon juice or a little vinegar and pinch of sugar. Add to plain Knox gelatine (half box dissolved in warm water), stir until it begins to congeal; mix together, serve on lettuce leaves with cooked mayonnaise with whipped cream in it

TOMATO AND SARDINE SALAD—Cut whole tomatoes in halves; sprinkle with shredded water cress and parsley; arrange one section of tomato and a sardine on a lettuce leaf and dress with cream mayonnaise

SAPSAGO SALAD—Grate a cake of sapsago cheese, mix the grated cheese with two tablespoons of butter, few drops Worcestershire sauce, and teaspoon lemon juice; mold into loaf, cut into strips, placing several on lettuce leaf, garnish with slices of red pepper or pickled beets. Serve with mayonnaise dressing if preferred.

WILTED LETTUCE SALAD—One head of lettuce washed and chopped fine. Have a hot skillet, cut up several pieces of bacon and when brown, pour one-half of vinegar and water into skillet; when all are hot pour over the lettuce, have two hard boiled eggs, slice one up in salad, the other over the top; serve at once before it gets cold.

COLD SLAW—Take head of cabbage, shave very fine with Irish potato chipper. Make dressing as follows: Two eggs, beaten, teaspoon sugar, pinch of salt and black pepper, two-thirds cup of vinegar, one spoon butter; cook until thick; sprinkle a little salt over slaw and pour your dressing over it, put in dish and garnish with hard boiled eggs. Lettuce is also nice fixed like this.

CHICKEN SALAD—Take one fat hen, boiled tender, eight hard boiled eggs, three bunches of celery; clip all fine with scissors. Cooked dressing for same: One-half cup vinegar, four eggs, yolks well beaten, one teaspoon salt, one of black pepper, one large kitchen spoon sugar, one pint cream. Let vinegar, sugar, salt and pepper come to boil, add it slowly to the well beaten eggs; set on warm part of stove and stir constantly; let all get cold, mix and add the pint of cream whipped.

DELICIOUS EASTERN SALAD—Boil three or four eggs until hard; remove yolks and cut in slices; rub yolks to a paste; gradually add to them, two tablespoons of olive oil or melted butter, two tablespoons of lemon juice; season with half teaspoon of salt and a dash of cayenne; rub into this dressing, lightly, one cup of grated cheese and a cupful of finely chopped chicken. Garnish with whites of eggs cut into rings; serve in lettuce leaves with tiny potato eggs on top.

ASPARAGUS SALAD—Take can asparagus tips and cut up with two buches of celery, one-half cup of pecans; salt and season to taste; mix with mayonnaise dressing.

PPLE RING SALAD—Pare and core two apples and slice them crosswise, brush them with lemon juice and dip each in French dressing, place the apple rings on lettuce leaves and put between them layers of chopped English walnuts and celery; put a ball of cream cheese on top and serve with mayonnaise dressing

IARINE SALAD—Scoop out the inside of unpeeled cucumbers, so that they resemble little green boats. Chop the pulp fine, add a little onion, drain, then add chopped peppers or celery Add French dressing A place card attached to a toothpick will give each of the boats a sail

OBSTER SALAD—Boil two lobsters, weighing four or five pounds each, when cold, remove the meat, being careful not to break the body or tail, shell and cut the meat into dice, clean the two tail shells and one back shell in cold water and with scissors remove the thin shell from the under side of tail. Place two or three layers of lettuce leaves around the salad dish; join the shells together in the form of a boat, the body shell in center and place them in the salad dish Mix the lobster meat with mayonnaise dressing and place in this boat, garnish with a chain of the whites of hard boiled eggs, cut into slices and linked together Serve at once.

ITTLE PIGS IN BLANKETS—Season large oysters with salt and pepper, cut bacon in very thin slices, wrap in each slice an oyster and fasten with a wooden toothpick, heat a frying pan and put in the little pigs. Cook just long enough to crisp the bacon, about two minutes. Place on small slices of toast and serve immediately. Do not remove the toothpick Garnish with parsley. The pan must be very hot before the pigs are put in and great care taken that they do not burn.

STUFFED LEMONS—Six lemons, soaked in soda water thirty minutes, then cut in halves and take out inside, take one can of sardines, three crackers, rolled fine, one-third cup of lemon juice, two pickles, grated, half teaspoon of sugar, one onion, grated, and four eggs boiled and grated, season with pepper and salt to suit the taste; mix thoroughly and stuff the lemons.

STUFFED ORANGES—One dozen oranges, cut in halves; remove the pulp and add to it, one pound each of English walnuts and blanched almonds, chopped fine; one cup of wine or grape juice, sweeten to taste, and put in hulls. Serve with whipped cream and cherries.

HEAVENLY HASH—Three oranges, one pound each of figs and dates, one-half can of pineapple, one pound of English walnuts; chop all fine; mix and serve with whipped cream.

HAZELNUT SALAD—Shell and blanch one pound of hazelnuts and grind half of them fine in a grinder. Grate half of pineapple; mix with the nuts and a tablespoonful of sherry; juice of half lemon and a tablespoonful of powdered sugar. Let stand one hour; then drain and add a package of cream cheese; mix to a paste; then make into balls with a whole nut in the center of each, put on white lettuce leaves and cover with mayonnaise.

EASTER SALAD—Salt and pepper one cup of cold boiled fowl cut into dice, and one cup chopped pecans, add one grated red pepper from which seeds have been removed, one cup celery cut into small pieces, mayonnaise to moisten. Trim crackers four inches long by one wide, using a sharp knife, salt slightly. Arrange on plate in form of box, keep in place with red ribbon one-half inch wide and fasten at corners by tying in a bow. Garnish opposite corners with sprig of holly berries. Line box with lettuce leaves, put in a spoonful of salad and mask with mayonnaise. Any colored ribbon may be used and flowers instead of berries.

EGG SALAD—Cut four hard boiled eggs in halves crosswise in such a way that tops of halves may be cut in small points, remove yolks and add an equal amount of finely chopped cooked chicken. Moisten with oil dressing No One Shape in balls of original yolks and refill whites. Arrange on lettuce leaves, garnish with radishes cut in fancy shapes and serve with mayonnaise.

OIL DRESSING—Four hard boiled eggs, four tablespoons oil, four tablespoons vinegar, one-half tablespoon sugar, one-half teaspoon mustard, one-half teaspoon salt, few grains cayenne, white of one egg Force yolks of hard boiled eggs through a strainer, then work until smooth, using a silver spoon Add sugar, mustard, salt and cayenne and when well mixed add gradually oil and vinegar, stirring and beating until thoroughly mixed, then cut and fold in whites of eggs beaten until stiff.

HARVARD SALAD—Make lemon baskets Make a hole through the handle of basket and insert a small sprig of parsley. Fill basket with equal parts of cold sweet breads and cucumber cut in small cubes and one-fourth the quantity of finely cut celery Moisten with mayonnaise. Pare round red radishes as thinly as possible, smooth top of basket and cover with dressing. Sprinkle top of one-half of basket with chopped parings, the remaining half with finely chopped parsley Arrange red and green baskets alternately on serving dish and garnish with water cress.

DAISY SALAD—Boil eggs hard, take out yolks and put through a strainer, cut lengthwise, cut each half in three pointed pieces. Put yolks in center of lettuce leaf and white pieces around like petals of a daisy. Serve mayonnaise with the dish

FRUIT SALAD—Mix one-half box of Cox's gelatine with one cup of pineapple juice, one-half cup of cold water. Let stand about two hours until thoroughly dissolved. Add one cup of boiling water, one of sugar, juice of two lemons and stir until all are dissolved. Strain all through coarse cloth, cut pineapple into small blocks, also three bananas and three oranges, using only the pulp of same, add as many California grapes as you wish, first removing the seed. When gelatine begins to congeal add fruit and serve with whipped cream.   Bananas may be left out if desired.

BANANA BOAT SALAD—Take one banana for one person. Strip peeling from one side being careful to leave it all around for one inch from end; this makes the boat.   Turn the side up that has the peeling off.   Put a small United States flag on one end, put seat in center of boat made of celery with a toy man on it; fill boat with any kind of salad made of fruit, and serve on lettuce or in long glass pickle dishes filled with water with leaves dropped around it and celery oars.

A NOAH'S ARK SALAD—Take large bell peppers, cut back about half way, take out the inside, fill the back part with salad of stuffed tomatoes found in this book or any other kind; make a float of celery on the front part like a gallery.   Put animal crackers around that, put up a little flag on the front.   Serve on lettuce leaves.

A ROSE TOMATO SALAD—Take a tomato, cut carefully at top, roll back carefully on each side from top and take seed out.   Let green English peas run down on four sides of inside of tomato.   One right on top of each other from bottom of tomato up to the top and drop a ball of mayonnaise down in center of tomato.   Serve on lettuce leaf. This makes a very pretty dish.

A RED AND WHITE FRUIT SALAD—One cup of boiled dressing, one-half cup of whipped cream, half   can   of white cherries, one small bottle of Maraschino cherries, one-half can of sliced pineapple, one cup of nuts.   Soak. one heaping tablespoon of gelatine and one-fourth cup of hot water.   Mix dressing and whipped cream together and gradually add cool gelatine. Cut fruit in small pieces, drain and dry on towel, sprinkle with salt and gently fold into the mixed fruit dressing, put in mold and allow to stand on ice for several hours.

GRAPE FRUIT SALAD—Three grape fruits, three small apples, two small bunches of celery, three bananas Cut all in small dice, mix all together with sugar enough to sweeten to taste, serve on lettuce leaves with mayonnaise.

A POINSETTA SALAD—Take one whole slice of pineapple, take red pimento and slice like little pennants Put the points on outer edge of pineapple and let wide part go to the inside It takes about seven little pennants to go around Let the wide part of pennants touch each other. Cut a lettuce leaf in half and roll it around and stick down in center hole of pineapple. Fill this little lettuce cup with mayonnaise and drop a red cherry right in top of mayonnaise. Fix one for each person like this Serve on lettuce leaves. This is beautiful.

MISCELLANEOUS

CHEESE SOUFFLE—One-quarter pound cheese, one-half pint of sweet milk, four eggs, beaten separately, three tablespoonsful flour, make the flour into a paste with a little of the milk and add to the well beaten yolks; then some of the beaten whites and cheese and milk until it is all used, add pepper and salt; bake slowly till firm.

APPLE SNOWBALL—Apple snowballs are a general favorite with children, and grown-ups like them equally as well. Peel and remove cores from juicy tart apples, fill the cavities with chopped raisins, sugar, mixed with cinnamon and butter, bake or stew until tender, in the meantime, boil some rice tender but not mushy, spread it an inch thick over small squares of coarse muslin; wet in cold water, in the center of each of these squares, put one of the apples, tie cloth carefully, being sure to have the apple covered with the rice, steam ten minutes, then remove the cloth and serve with lemon or maple sugar sauce.

CHEESE BALLS IN RICE NEST—Mix with one and a half cupsful of cream cheese, one tablespoonful of flour, one-third teaspoonful salt, a little mustard and small pinch of cayenne pepper, mix these well together, then whip in the whites of three well beaten eggs, form in egg shape, about the size of large bird eggs, roll in whites of an egg, then in cracker crumbs, fry quickly in deep fat, make nests of seasoned cooked rice and place three cheese eggs in each nest

CHINESE DUMPLINGS—Put a quart of ripe tomatoes into a shallow dish, add seasoning of salt, cayenne pepper and a little butter; cover and let get boiling hot, add tiny bit of chopped onion, meanwhile, make a drop batter with two cups of sifted flour, two teaspoons Royal Baking Powder, one-half teaspoon salt and sufficient water to make batter that will drop from a spoon; add a cup of highly seasoned cooked meats to batter and drop from a spoon on top of the boiling tomato; cover closely and steam for twenty minutes, serve dumplings as a border around tomato

JAMBAYLAY—Fine. Take a tablespoonful of butter, put in a hot skillet, chop up one slice of ham, either cooked or raw, and one onion; fry all together till brown but be careful not to burn, take one cup of rice, wash and put in pan; strain one can of tomatoes into rice, fill pan with enough water to cook rice done without stirring. Pour your fried mixture into rice; season highly with red pepper and a good deal of salt; mix all together and don't disturb any more until done; let cook on top of stove until nearly dry. Then run into the stove and brown. Be sure to put enough salt as the tomatoes kill the salt and it takes a good deal; use more rice if you have a large crowd.

ARTIFICIAL BRAINS—Take one-half pint of cold pork roast, ground fine, put on to cook in barely enough water to cover; season highly with salt and pepper; stir into this three well beaten eggs and you will have a dish that can't be detected from real brains

JAMBAYLAY FOR SMALL FAMILIES—Take three dozen oysters, stew them in their liquor, then chop fine and add one beaten egg, cold cooked pork sausage; Edam cheese, grated; rice, butter, salt and pepper, sweet milk and onions, stir all these well together, then pour over the mixture the liquor in which the oysters were stewed and cook consistency of boiled rice, turkey or chicken is often substituted for the sausage; put in a little red pepper.

CHEESE BALLS—One-half pound grated cheese, one-half pound butter; melt, pour over cheese and mix thoroughly, adding salt and a dash of red pepper; mold into balls the size of walnuts, press a walnut meat on each side; keep cool until ready to use These balls are very nice for luncheon

WELCH RAREBIT—One cup of milk, let it get hot, one-fourth pound cheese, one-half teaspoon of salt, one-fourth teaspoon of mustard, one tablespoon flour; rub butter and flour together, last, beat one egg and add little at a time until smooth, serve at once on crackers

ITALIAN SPAGHETTI—Two pounds of beef and two slices of bacon

SAUCE FOR SAME—One can tomatoes, strained, six finely chopped onions, size of egg, one teaspoon finely chopped garlic, one of salt, one-fourth teaspoon red pepper, one of thyme, one tablespoon of flour, for thickening paste, one of butter, one of grated cheese Fry meat brown, then boil till tender to get substance out, pour sauce on meats; add one quart water, and continue to add water as sauce boils away, cooking well, till onions are tender, or about three hours. Add thickening and chees. Put three-fourths pound of spaghetti in boiling water, add one teaspoon salt and boil twenty minutes, drain off and put sauce over it; let stand about five minutes, serve with Italian cheese grated over it.

CHEESE STRAWS—One cup grated cheese, three-fourths cup butter, one cup flour, one-half teaspoon salt, one-half teaspoon red pepper, mixed with the juice of lemon. Bake a delicate brown

SHIRRED EGGS—One tablespoonful butter, two eggs, salt and pepper to taste, melt butter in chafing dish over slow heat so it will not brown, break eggs into chafing dish and season; serve with fried crumbs and parsley sprinkled on grated cheese

BAKED OMELET—Have ready a well buttered baking dish, or small granite baker ; for a family of six, take four eggs, one teacup of sweet milk, butter, size of walnut, one-half teaspoonful of salt, three tablespoons of grated cheese, or more if desired; separate eggs, beat each well, add milk, butter, salt and cheese to beaten yolks, then stir the well beaten whites into mixture, pour into baking dish and brown quickly, serving at once

CREAM OMELET—One tablespoon of pure cream for each egg, one teaspoon of grated cheese for each of cream; melt one spoon of butter; when hot, mix the ingredients well and pour in as the omelet begins to set, roll up and serve at once on hot dish; season with salt and pepper to taste

SMOTHERED EGGS—Take the required number of hard boiled eggs, one for each person to be served, mix some mashed potatoes with half its bulk of finely chopped meat of any kind, and bind with beaten eggs; divide this into as many parts as people to be served, and roll each portion around a hard boiled egg after removing shell, of course, lay in well greased pan and add gravy, if there is any left, if not, tomato dressing, and bake twenty minutes in hot oven or until brown

CHILI CON CARNE—One round steak, ground, one table-spoon of lard, half of a medimum-sized onion, six cloves or garlic, six chili peppers, pinch of salt. Take seed out of peppers, boil peppers in water and they will skin easily Chop fine and add to the meat

MEXICAN CHILI NO. 1—One pound chopped beef, one tablespoon of chili, small onion, two small potatoes, half can tomatoes Put chili in cup of hot water; let stand until beef and potatoes are done, then pour in and boil together.

MEXICAN CHILI NO. 2—Chop one pound of beef into small pieces; fry till brown two tablespoons of lard; add three pints of water and Eagle chili powder to suit the taste. Boil thirty minutes.

—73—

CHILI CON CARNE—Put two tablespoons of lard in a kettle and let heat, then add one pound of ground chili meat, cooked five minutes, stirring constantly, then add one quart of water, three pods of chili pepper, removing seed, one tablespoon camena seed; add water and cook well.

STUFFED EGGS—Boil one dozen eggs until hard, cut in halves, take yolks out and mash the yellows to a cream; add a lump of butter, salt and pepper to taste, little mustard and tiny bit of ground celery seed, and a small box of potted ham; mix all together and stuff back into the whites.

WELSH RAREBIT—Boil one cup of milk, tablespoon of mustard, cayenne pepper to taste; into this, put one pound of grated cheese, the yolks of four well beaten eggs; when thick and smooth pour over toasted bread or crackers. Serve very hot.

HOME-MADE LYE HOMINY—Take one quart of big cracked hominy, put in pot full of water; after it commences to boil, add one teaspoonful of soda; stir often and cook slowly till done. If it gets too dry before done, add a little more water. When done, put a tablespoon of grease in skillet, if too dry add a little more water; mash as much of your hominy as you need for a meal, salt and pepper to taste and fry. Put the balance in refrigerator for future use. You cannot tell this from the old-fashioned lye hominy.

SPANISH TONGUE—Boil a beef tongue until tender, take off the outer skin, then rub with the beaten yolk of an egg. Put in a baking dish; add one-half cup of water in which the tongue was cooked, one-half glass of wine and one-half can of mushrooms; sprinkle with salt and pepper and let bake until brown; serve, garnish with the mushrooms.

VEAL LOAF—Three pounds of beefsteak, ground, six crackers pulverized, three eggs, two tablespoons of butter one teaspoon of pepper, one-half teaspoon pulverized sage (if liked). one teaspoon of salt. Make into pone and bake brown. Make a tomato sauce and pour over it and cook a while in it. Put a little ground onion in your loaf, too

OX EYE EGGS—Take pieces of nicely browned toast, dip each piece in a pan of hot milk, and arrange as many pieces on a dish as you have people to serve. Take as many eggs as pieces of toast and separate, being careful not to break the yolks. Every yolk should be put into a saucer by itself. Beat the whites to a stiff froth, put some on every piece of toast and drop one yolk down in the middle of the whites on toast, sprinkle each with salt, put a pea of butter on each yolk, set dish on stove till whites are slightly browned, arrange around dish with parsley

EGGS A LA ENGLISH—Fix English peas in a pan with cream dressing the usual way, break your eggs right into the pan with your peas and let them poach; have nicely browned bread and lift them out and serve on toast with peas sticking over the eggs with melted butter poured over each piece. Have a good deal of dressing in pan with peas

POTATO SOMERSET STYLE—Two cups hot diced potatoes, two tablespoons butter, one-half cup grated cheese, yolks three eggs slightly beaten, one-half teaspoon salt and a few grains cayenne pepper. Shape in form of birds, dip in crumbs, egg the crumbs, insert pieces of raw potato cut to represent wings and tail, and cloves to represent eyes. Fry in deep fat and drain on brown paper

POTATO NESTS—Wash, pare and cut potatoes in thin strips, using same slicer as for lattice potatoes, soak in cold water fifteen minutes, drain and dry between towels. Line a fine strainer of four inch diameter having a wire handle, with potatoes, place a similar strainer having a two and one-half inch diameter in larger strainer, thus holding potatoes in nest shapes. Fry in deep fat taking

—75—

care that the fat does not reach too high a temperature at first. Keep the small strainer in place during frying with a long handled spoon. Carefully remove nests from strainer, drain on brown paper and sprinkle with salt Fill with small fillets of fried fish.

CHEESE STRAWS—Roll puff or plain paste one-fourth of an inch thick, sprinkle one-half with grated cheese to which has been added a few grains of salt and cayenne pepper. Fold, press edges firmly together, fold again, pat and roll out one-fourth inch thick Sprinkle with cheese and proceed as before. Repeat twice; cut in strips five inches long and one-fourth wide Bake eight minutes in a hot oven Cheese straws are piled log cabin style and served with cheese or salad course.

HAM SOUFFLE—Two tablespoons butter, two flour, one and one-half cups sweet milk, three eggs, tablespoon chili sauce, one tablespoon grated cheese, one cup ground ham, salt and cayenne pepper to season. Melt the butter and add the flour and stir until smooth Heat milk and gradually pour into flour mixture, stirring constantly until it thickens Remove from the fire and add the beaten yolks of eggs, chili sauce, cheese and seasoning. Set aside to cool and when cold stir in ham and fold in the stiffly beaten whites of eggs. Pour into a well buttered and hot baking dish Bake in a moderately hot oven until firm in the center. Garnish with parsley or water cress and serve immediately.

CHEESE SOUFFLE—Make a white sauce using two tablespoons fat, three tablespoons flour, one-half teaspoon salt, speck of cayenne and one-half cup of milk. Add one-half cup grated cheese. Fold in the beaten yolks of three eggs, then fold in the beaten whites. Pour into a greased baking dish that will fit the cooker rack Regulate heat till testing paper browns in forty-five seconds. Bake forty minutes.

SPANISH OMELET—Put two tablespoonsful oil into a frying pan and fry in it a tablespoon of chopped green peppers, one of onion and one of chopped olives, add three good sized tomatoes ad stew gently until the sauce is rich and thick. Beat six eggs until light, season with salt and pepper and turn into the omelet pan. When the omelet is well settled and about done pour sauce in the middle and fold over, or place the sauce around the omelet Green peas added make a nice garnish

POTAOTO OMELET WITH BACON STRIPS—Fry several thin slices of bacon, take four cups boiled Irish potatoes, one cup of sweet milk, salt and pepper to taste, one tablespoon chopped parsley Pour in skillet where bacon was fried, brown nicely and turn like an omelet Serve on dish with bacon strips arranged on omelet.

ICES

TUTTI FRUITTI CREAM—One quart water, juice of three lemons; one can grated pineapple; three or four large oranges, cut into small pieces; six bananas, sliced fine, three or four soft peaches; add sugar until very sweet, add whites of well beaten eggs and freeze.

BRULE ICE CREAM—Two quarts milk, two cups sugar and six eggs; mix milk and one-half of sugar together; put other half sugar into kettle to dissolve on stove; when it begins to turn brown pour into custard and boil until thick; when cool, add one pint rich cream and freeze at once.

OLD FASHIONED BOILED CUSTARD ICE CREAM— Take three quarts of sweet milk, eight eggs, beaten separately; two cups sugar and one-half cup of flour, sifted into the sugar; beat flour, sugar and eggs together until light; then, add the whites beaten to a stiff froth; mix all together and pour into the hot milk, which should be boiled in a double boiler or bucket; set in a pan of water. Let cook until thick, flavor with lemon or vanilla.

GRAPE JUICE SHERBET—Make one gallon lemonade and add one pint grape juice and one quart milk. Sweeten to taste and freeze.

PROVIDENCE FROZEN FIG PUDDING—One pint milk, one-half cup each dates, figs, and English walnuts, chopped fine, one-half cup sugar, two eggs and one teaspoon vanilla. Beat eggs, milk and sugar together and cook until it thickens. When nearly cool stir in the dates, figs and nuts; add vanilla and freeze.

CRANBERRY PUNCH—Two quarts of cranberries, sweetened to taste, cooked and put through a collander, add a glass of good brandy and enough water to make a gallon of ice and freeze. Nice with turkey course.

PUNCH—Put a pint of water, the chopped rind of a lemon and a pound of sugar on to boil; boil five minutes, remove from fire and allow to cool, when ready to serve, add the juice of eight lemons, a can of grated pineapple, a can of cherries and Appollinaris water, or plain water if preferred, sufficient to serve.

CHERRY MOUSSE—Soak one-fourth box gelatine in one-half cup of warm water until dissolved, whip one pint of cream, add gelatine and one cup of crystalized cherries and sweeten to taste. Put in a mold and pack in ice and salt until it begins to stiffen, stirring frequently to prevent cherries from settling, let stand about two hours before serving.

FRUIT PUNCH—Two dozen lemons, one-half jar of Maraschino cherries, six oranges, one can of cherries, two cans pineapple, cut in pieces, one can of grapes, one box strawberries, one gallon of Appollinaris water; sweeten to taste, put in juice of the canned fruit, put into this a large block of ice.

ORANGE SHERBET—Juice of six lemons, juice of eight oranges, one pint box of grated pineapple, three quarts of water, sweeten to taste and freeze.

PINEAPPLE SHERBET—One can of grated pineapples; pour two quarts of boiling water over it and add five cups of sugar, juice of ten lemons, leave the rind in until cool, then take the rinds out and add the whites of three eggs, well beaten and one quart of milk, freeze as soon as you put the milk in. This is fine.

GRAPE ICE—One quart of grape juice, one cup of orange juice, make sweet, white of one egg beaten stiff. Freeze.

STRAWBERRY ICE—For one gallon of strawberry ice, use two boxes of berries, pick and wash, three cups of sugar, one quart of cream, two tablespoons of gelatine, one pint of water, whites of two eggs. Dissolve Knox gelatine in a little cold water; to the sugar, add the pint of water and set on the stove to boil; add dissolved gelatine and let boil a few minutes longer; set off to cool; then add the crushed berries; then the cream and put into the freezer; after it begins to freeze add the whites of two eggs well beaten. The juice of two lemons will improve it.

FROZEN GRAPE ICE—To a quart of grape juice, add a pint of water; sweeten to taste and when about frozen, add the whites of two eggs beaten to a stiff froth; continue the freezing process until the eggs and ice are thoroughly mixed and hard frozen; set for an hour or more. This amount, when properly mixed, will fill a six-quart freezer; if preferred, a lemon may be added in making the ice; this is delicious.

ICED APRICOT—One can of apricots, one quart of water, lemon, one orange, yolk of one egg, three cups of sugar; dissolve sugar in water and boil to a syrup; when cool, add the orange, lemon, and can of apricots with the skin removed and mashed up; freeze; it is fine with a cup of cream added.

ANGEL ICE—Three pints of thick cream; before whipping, add one cup of sherry wine; whip to a stiff froth and place on ice. The whites of four eggs, beaten stiff, one pint of sugar; pour enough of water over sugar to dissolve and cook as for icing; beat into the eggs; then fold the cream in the eggs and sugar, pack in freezer and let stand three or four hours.

BLACKBERRY ACID—Three gallons blackberries, two gallons water (boiling), let stand twenty-four hours; strain then add to every three pints of juice, two pounds of sugar, three ounces tartaric acid to the whole, let stand twenty-four hours; strain and bottle; put up hot or cold.

BLACKBERRY CORDIAL—One quart blackberry juice, one pound of sugar, mace, cloves, allspice and cinnamon to taste; boil until thick and strain through a sieve when cold; to every gallon of juice, add a quart of brandy.

STRAWBERRY COCKTAIL—One quart strawberries, one quart sugar, wash and cap berries, sprinkle with sugar, let stand an hour, mash fine and put in cocktail glasses and serve with one spoon of pineapple sherbet colored green.

PICKLES

MIXED PICKLE—Two gallons chopped cabbage and green tomatoes, one gallon each, one pint of chopped onions; sprinkle well with salt and let stand all night; next morning, squeeze out the brine, put in your kettle with five tablespoons of mustard, three gills of white mustard seed, two tablespoons of ground black pepper, two of allspice, two teaspoons ground cloves, one pound brown sugar, one tablespoon of celery seed, one tablespoon of tumeric, mix all these well with vinegar, then mix with cabbage and tomatoes, add three quarts best cider vinegar; put all on stove, cook well about three-quarters of an hour

SWEET PEACH PICKLE—Seven pounds of fruit three and a half pounds sugar, one quart of vinegar, stick three cloves in each peach, put on vinegar and sugar; when very hot, drop in fruit, when tender put in jars

CABBAGE PICKLE—Put cabbage in brine for a week, then take out, put in weak vinegar to take out salt, let remain in vinegar twenty-four hours, it is then ready for the pickle, which is made in the following manner. To one gallon of vinegar put two pounds of sugar, three ounces of tumeric, some ground mustard, one teacup of white mustard seed, one teacup of black pepper seed, two whole peppers, celery seed, one tablespoon each of cloves, spice, pepper and mace, two nutmegs grated, pour all in boiler, let boil, when cold pour over cabbage

CHOW CHOW PICKLE—Take one and a half pecks green tomatoes, one and a half dozen onions, three heads cabbage, one dozen green peppers two dozen red peppers and chop as desired, sprinkle half pint salt over them, put them in a thin domestic bag; let drain all night; put in granite kettle or pan with two pounds sugar, one and one-half grated horse radish, one tablespoon each of ground black pepper, ground mustard, white mustard, mace, celery seed; cover all with vinegar and let boil till clear.

GREEN BELL PEPPER CATSUP—Take one hundred pods of green pepper, one gallon of vinegar, boil together till soft enough to strain or press through a sieve; then add two tablespoons white mustard seed, ground, three tablespoons of salt, one of black pepper, small cup of sugar and half pint of onions chopped fine; add spice and celery seed to suit the taste. Boil until onions are well cooked and bottle tight; this is fine on meats

TOMATO CATSUP—To every gallon of tomatoes, sliced, add five tablespoonsful of salt, two of cayenne, and two of black pepper, one teaspoon of mace, one of cinnamon, one-half teaspoon cloves, two large onions, sliced, one tumbler full of good brown sugar, one quart of good apple vinegar, one tablespoon of mustard; stir often, cook four hours, bottle when cold. This is excellent.

CHILI SAUCE—Thirty-six ripe tomatoes, one can may be used, eight medium sized onions, twelve green peppers, eight tablespoons of sugar, seven level of salt, eight small teacups of vinegar, put all in kettle, chop up well, add one teaspoon each of ground cloves, spice, mace, nutmeg, black and red pepper. One tablespoon of Coleman's mustard, cooked till thick, which generally requires three or four hours, stir constantly to prevent scorching. This never spoils if cooked enough and sealed tightly

SALAD RELISH—Two quarts green tomatoes, chopped fine, measure all ingredients after chopping fine, one quart of onions, nine quarts of bell pepper, eight quarts of hot pepper, mix and cook with cold water; add half cup of salt and boil tender. Dressing: If vinegar is very strong, dilute with a little water and use two quarts, three cups of sugar, one of flour, ten tablespoons of mustard, five cents worth of tumeric; mix well, commencing with just a little vinegar; boil in double boiler until consistency of cream; then add one quart of chopped, sour cucumber pickles; pour over the other mixture and boil a little while; seal like fruit This makes fine sandwiches, mixed with ground meat

PIMENTOS—Take one pint of cooking oil for a small amount and season with vinegar to taste, add salt and red pepper to taste. Put the cooking oil and vinegar on stove and let come to a boil, then add the big red bell pepper and let them boil just a little Put the whole in a jar and seal tightly.

A SWEET TOMATO PICKLE—Seven pounds sliced tomatoes, (green), four pounds sugar, three quarts of vinegar, one pound seeded raisins, cinnamon two teaspoons, spice two teaspoons, cloves two teaspoons Soak tomatoes in bucket of water with a teacup of lime in it two or three hours, then drain off and soak a while in a little fresh water. Boil all together about two hours Don't add the raisins until nearly done, add a little salt to taste before cooking

A MIXED PICKLE—Two quarts of green tomatoes, one quart of red tomatoes; after scalding and taking peeling off, add three small bunches of celery chopped fine or two tablespoons of celery seed; three large onions, three red sweet peppers, three green sweet peppers, leaving out seed part. One small head of cabbage, one ripe cucumber, half a cup of salt. Chop the vegetables, cover them with salt, and let stand over night. Drain well next morning. Add three pints of vinegar, two pounds of brown sugar, one teaspoon of mustard, one teaspoon of black pepper. Cook until clear about an hour and three-quarters. Let cool and seal in jar.

PRESERVES, JELLIES AND CANNED FRUITS

FIG PRESERVES—Take figs not quite ripe enough to eat, don't peel or pull stems off, put them in a bucket of cold water and pour one-half teacup of lime in water and stir up; let the figs stand in this water one hour (this keeps them from mashing up), then rinse them in another bucket of pure water, then weigh them; put three-quarters of a pound of sugar to every pound of fruit; let boil until syrup is pretty thick. When you first put the figs and sugar on to cook, pour just enough water over it to keep from burning

PEAR PRESERVES—Take pears, peel, quarter and remove all core; measure three-quarters pound sugar to one pound of fruit, put sugar over fruit and let stand all night; next morning cook until syrup is thick; put in a sliced lemon if preferred.

STRAWBERRY PRESERVES—To every quart of berries, use one quart of sugar, boil each quart of berries and sugar in a pan to itself, boil hard for twenty minutes and then seal in a tight jar while hot. Fix each quart of berries and sugar this way. You will find it easier and better than the old way of boiling them all together at once.

PLUM PRESERVES—Take one pound of sugar to each pound of plums and cook until done.

MUSCADINE PRESERVES—Wash the muscadines; separate the hulls and pulp and boil the hulls until tender in barely enough water to cover them; boil the pulps in a little water and mash through a sifter to extract seed, add pulp to hulls, then add one pound of sugar to one of fruit; boil steadily thirty minutes or until well done.

BLACKBERRY JAM—Take berries, wash and put three-quarters of a pound of sugar to one pound of fruit; boil until thick, put a little water over fruit to start cooking.

WILD PLUM JELLY—Take wild plums, wash and put in kettle to boil, cover with water; boil until mushy; take off; cool and strain through a thin domestic bag; take a cup of sugar and a cup of juice until it is all measured; let boil till it will jelly when cooled in a saucer, keep trying it until done, pour into jelly glasses while hot. By recooking for a short time, the plums may be used to get more juice and more jelly made from them, almost as much as from the first squeezing.

CANNED PEACHES—Take peaches, peel and quarter them off the seed, weigh and put one-quarter pound of sugar to one pound of fruit, let stand all night with sugar over it; next morning, boil until you can stick a straw through them, put in jars while hot and seal. Be sure your rubbers are on air tight.

BRANDIED PEACHES—Put the peaches in boiling water for a few minutes so the skin will peel off easily, make a syrup of one-half pound of sugar to one-half cup of water to each pound of peaches; skim as skum rises in boiling; then put in peaches and boil gently till tender, and no longer. Take them out carefully and fill jars; remove the syrup from fire and add to it half pint of brandy to every pound of peaches. The peaches should be two-thirds ripe.

CRANBERRY JELLY—Pick and wash the cranberries thoroughly, put on to cook with enough water to cover, let boil until tender then add sugar enough to sweeten to taste, cook until it will jelly in a saucer when cooled, take off, rub through a sifter into a bowl, when cool slice and serve with fowl or other meats

THE ART OF DRYING
AND CANNING

The cold pack method of canning is so simple and the instructions so easily followed that the women of the country are taking up the work by the thousands, says the National Emergency Food Garden Commission

In the cold pack method these are the steps taken

1.—Select sound vegetables and fruits It possible can them the same day they are picked Wash, clean and prepare them

2.—Have ready on the stove, can or pail of boiling water.

3.—Place the vegetables or fruits in cheesecloth or in some other porous receptacle—a wire basket is excellent—for dipping and blanching them in boiling water

4.—Put them whole into the boiling water After the water begins to boil begin to count the blanching time

5.—The blanching time varies from one to 20 minutes, according to the vegetable or fruit When the blanching is complete remove the vegetables or fruits from the boiling water and plunge them a number of times into cold water, to harden the pulp and check the flow of coloring matter Do not allow to stand in cold water

6.—The containers should be thoroughly clean It is not necessary to sterilize them in steam or boiling water before filling them for the reason that in the cold pack process both the insides of containers and the contents are sterilized The jars should be heated before the cold product is put in them

7.—Pack the product into the containers, leaving about a quarter of an inch of space at the top.

8 —With vegetables add one level teaspoon of salt to each quart container and fill with boiling water. With fruits use syrups.

9.—With glass jars always use a new rubber. Test the rubber by stretching or turning inside out. Fit on the rubber and put the lid in place If the container has a screw, twist it up as hard as possible, but use only the thumb and little finger in tightening it. This makes it possible for steam generated within to escape and prevents breakage If a glass top jar is used snap the top bail only, leaving the lower bail loose during sterilization. Tin cans should be completely sealed.

10 —Place the filled and capped containers on the rack in the sterilizer. If the home-made or commercial hot water bath outfit is used some authorities insist that enough water should be in the boiler to come at least one inch above the tops of the containers, and that the water, in boiling out, should never be allowed to drop to the level of these tops Begin to count processing time when the water begins to boil

11 —At the end of the sterilizing period remove the containers from the sterilizer. Fasten covers on tightly at once, tip each container over to test for leakage, and store Be sure that no draught is allowed to blow on glass jars, as it may cause breakage.

12 —If jars are to be stored where there is strong light wrap them in paper, preferable brown, as light will fade the color of products canned in glass jars, and sometimes deteriorate the food value.

Vegetables are blanched before being put up for three purposes—to eliminate objectionable acids, to set coloring matter and to make texture firm for sterilization.

The object of the cold dip is to separate the skin and harden the pulp, to set color bodies and to render packing easier.

These recipes are recommended by the U. S government.

TOMATOES—Grade according to ripeness, size and equality Scald to loosen the skins Dip in cold water and remove the skin. Pack whole Fill with tomatoes only and add one level teaspoonful salt to each quart Place the rubber and partly seal. Sterilize 22 minutes in the hot water bath Remove the jars, tighten the covers, test the joints and invert to cool

CARROTS, PARSNIPS, SWEET POTATOES, ETC.—Scald from one to five minutes in boiling water Plunge in cold water Remove skins, pack whole or sliced, add boiling water and one level teaspoons salt to each quart Place rubber and top, then partly tighten Leave one and one-half hours in hot water bath

EGG PLANT—Scald five minutes in boiling salty water, plunge in cold water; remove skin Slice crosswise and pack, add boiling water and one level teaspoonful salt for to each pint. Place rubber and top, then partly tighten. Leave one hour in hot water bath Remove jars, tighten covers and invert to cool

SWEET CORN—On the Cob—Blanch in boiling water 10 to 15 minutes, according to ripeness, size and freshness; plunge in cold water Pack, alternating buts and tips; add just a little boiling water and one level teaspoonful of salt to each quart Place rubber and top and partly tighten Sterilize one and a half hours in water-seal outfit Remove jars, tighten covers, invert and cool (Heat up for table use in steamer, not in water.)

SWEET CORN—Off the Cob—Same as the foregoing recipe, except cut from ear after blanching Pack and fill jars with boiling water, adding one level teaspoon salt to each pint Proceed as before.

PEAS, BEANS, OKRA, ETC.—Blanch five to 10 minutes in boiling water; plunge in cold water. Pack and add boiling water and one level teaspoonful salt to each pint. Place rubber and top, then partly tighten top. Process one and one-half hours in hot water bath.

—89—

BEETS, TURNIPS, ETC.—Blanch one to 10 minutes in boiling water; plunge in cold water, remove skins. Slice and pack; add boiling water and one level teaspoonful salf for each pint Place rubber and top and partly tighten. Process one and one-half hours in hot water bath Remove jars, tighten covers and invert to cool

GREENS—(Spinach, Dandelions, Mustard, Beet Tops, Swiss Chard)—Blanch in boiling water 10 to 20 minutes, plunge in cold water Cut ready for table use Season with slice of bacon for each pint. Pack, add hot water and a little salt to each quart. Place rubber and top and partly tighten. Process 90 minutes in hot water bath. Remove, tighten covers and invert to cool It is always advisable to process the greens a short time before packing in order to reduce the bulk or make possible a full pack

Great results are expected from the dehydrating processes, which have been much improved and are being made use of more extensively this year than ever before One of the kind which may be used in private houses is in daily operation at the depot in Hicksville, L. I. Here on three days of the week garden and farm products are preserved under comteptent instructors and will be stored and sold under the direction of the Long Island Food Battalion. On the other three week days the kitchen is open to women of the district who wish to preserve their own fruit and vegetables.

All kinds of vegetables may be dried They must be washed and, those that require it, peeled and sliced. Modern drying is not the tedious process that it was in other times Small quantities can be sufficiently dried in from two to four hours, according to the degree of succulence. They not only retain their flavor but much of their color, and when put in water to soak for cooking have all the value of fresh vegetables. Not only is there a great saving in money in preserving fruits and vegetables in this way, but they require less room for storage and will keep almost indefinitely.

CANDIES

ENGLISH TOFFEE CANDY—Three cups dark brown sugar, one can condensed milk (Dime Brand) butter, size of an egg; mix sugar, milk and butter, place on fire and stir constantly and let the sugar melt thoroughly; cook till it threads or hardens in cold water; beat thoroughly and add one cup of pecans or walnuts, pour on dish and cut in squares   This needs no flavoring

HEAVENLY HASH CANDY—One pint white sugar, one pint brown sugar, one pint of milk and water mixed, two tablespoons butter, chocolate to color; cook until it will harden in water, and add one-fourth pound dates, figs, cocoanut and nuts to suit the taste   Chop fruit and nuts fine, beat candy until it begins to harden, then pour on a tin and cut in squares.

MARSHMALLOW CANDY—Dissolve one box Knox gelatine in one brimming cup of lukewarm water for one hour; soak four cups sugar in one and one-third cups of water and cook like icing.   When done, pour syrup over gelatine and flavor with vanilla   Beat forty minutes; when very stiff pour on a dish that has been buttered and the surface covered with powdered sugar, cut in squares and roll in powdered sugar   Put on plates to dry.

PEANUT CRISP—Take two cups of granulated sugar and one cup of peanuts, chopped slightly   Put sugar, without any water, into iron pan or skillet and stir until it melts, then pour over nuts which have been placed in buttered dish

PENOTCHIE CANDY—Take three cups light brown sugar and a cup of milk; boil until when dropped into water will form soft ball   Add a teaspoon of butter and remove from fire.   Add teaspoon of vanilla and a cup of English walnuts, meats broken fine   Stir until candy begins to cream, then pour it quickly into a buttered dish, making it the same thickness as for fudge   Tried once, this is a prime favorite.

OLD FASHIONED BUTTER SCOTCH—Two cups brown sugar, one-half cup butter, four tablespoons molasses, two of water, two of vinegar.   Put into a porcelain kettle; stir over fire until sugar is dissolved   Then boil without stirring until it hardens when dropped into cold water, pour into shallow buttered pan to cool, and when firm, mark off into squares; when cold, break off on lines.

CARAMEL CREAMS—Two cups brown sugar, one cup cream, butter, size of walnut, cook as for fudge; add one cup of English walnuts, pour into a buttered pan; when cold cut into squares.

DIVINITY FUDGE—Two and two-thirds cups sugar, two-thirds cup corn syrup, two-thirds cup of water, whites of two eggs, and one cup chopped up pecans.   Put sugar, water, and corn syrup on, and let boil until it is hard when dropped in cup of cold water   Have whites of eggs, beaten very stiff, and then beat the candy mixture with them; stir in nuts and flavor with vanilla, and beat until it begins to stiffen; pour into buttered dish and cut in squares

CREAM WALNUTS—Dissolve one pound of powdered sugar in half cup of water; boil five minutes and cool slowly, keeping it constantly stirred, and flavor.   When cold, if not stiff enough to handle, work in a little more sugar, roll into balls, press half of an English walnut on each side and drop into granulated sugar

CLUB CANDY—Three cups of sugar, one-half cup milk; cook until it forms a stiff ball in water, take from fire and beat in one-half dozen marshmallows, cut in pieces; one cup grated cocoanut, one-half cup each raisins and nuts chopped fine; pour in buttered tins and cut in squares

SNOW BALLS—Stuff seedless dates with marshmallows and peaches; dip in plain icing and at once roll in cocoanut.

COCOANUT CANDY—Boil together three cups of granulated sugar, one-half cup of water, one-half teaspoon cream of tartar; boil ten minutes and add a cup of grated cocoanut; when cool cut in squares.

FONDANT—Two cups of granulated sugar, one of water, and a scant quarter of a teaspoon of cream of tartar. Never stir after putting on fire. When it begins to look syrupy, stir a few drops in a saucer, if it creams, the candy is done; pour out and stir until cool enough to work with hands; the more it is worked the creamier it gets.

CANDIED POP CORN—Put into an iron kettle, one tablespoon of butter, three tablespoons of water, one cup of white sugar, boil until ready to candy; then throw in three quarts of nicely popped corn, stir briskly till candy is evenly distributed over corn; take kettle from fire, stir until it is cooled a little and you have each grain separate crystalized with sugar, taking care that corn does not burn Nuts of any kind prepared in this way are good.

CARAMEL CANDY—Take two cups of sugar and one cup sweet milk, put in vessel with teaspoon of butter and let cook slowly. Put one cup of sugar in at same time in a skillet and let brown, stir constantly until it all dissolves; then pour the brown sugar into the other and stir until all of the lumps dissolve Have a cup of pecans cut up. When candy strikes hard on side of cup in cold water, it is done Take up, flavor with vanilla, and beat pecans into mixture Pour on dish and cut into squares.

DATE LOAF—Two cups sugar, one cup sweet milk, one tablespoon Karo Corn Syrup, one package of dates two cups chopped pecans, one tablespoon butter Cook sugar and milk until it forms a soft ball when dropped in cold water, then add butter and dates chopped fine, stir until dates melt, then beat until it begins to harden, adding nuts and pour the whole into a wet napkin and roll up. When cold, slice end ways like a cake

LIGHT DIET FOR
THE SICK

HYGENIC EGG—Butter an ordinary glass, fill with the white of one egg beaten light, put yolk on the top and season with a little butter, salt and pepper and put glass into a covered vessel of steaming water until cooked.

PANNADA—Take dry bread and toast and cut in small squares, add sugar and nutmeg to taste, cover with hot water and serve.

LEMON ALBUMEN—Take the juice of half o lemon, white of one egg, add sugar to taste, put all together in a jar and shake well; add a small glass of water and strain.

BOILED FLOUR FOR SUMMER COMPLAINT IN CHILDREN OR FOR INVALIDS—Put a pint of flour in a clean sack or pudding bag, tie and place in pot of boiling water, boil eight hours; when done peel off the outer layer and you will have a hard white lump of flour, milk thickened with some of this flour grated makes a good gruel, can be sweetened or salted to taste. Can be eaten in small pieces as one would eat candy, and is excellent in bowel trouble.

SURE CURE FOR FLUX—Get the root of the common blackberry vine, scrape off the bark, place root in water and steep as in making tea, drink freely; it will also cure summer complaint in teething children and is harmless.

WHEN BOILING MILK—If pans in which milk, custards, or salad dressing are to be boiled are first wiped out with a cloth greased with lard they will neither stick nor scorch.

HOUSEHOLD HINTS

TO EXTRACT A SPLINTER—Take a wide-mouthed bottle and almost fill with hot water, then place the part with the splinter over the mouth of bottle and press lightly; the suction will draw the flesh from the splinter and the splinter may be easily removed. This also heals the soreness of the wound.

TO REMOVE INK SPOTS FROM WHITE GOODS—Dip in kerosene oil and rub with ordinary laundry soap, at the end of half an hour wash with soap and water

HOME-MADE FLOOR FINISH—To keep my hard wood and varnished floors in good condition, I take equal parts of linseed oil and coal oil, heat and rub floors. They will look like new. This makes a finish for any floor if brushed on while boiling hot

TO CLEAN RUGS—Rugs of a light color may be made to look almost like new in the following way. Beat thoroughly and, after the dust has settled, spread over the rug, a paste of corn meal and gasoline. Rub in with a clean stiff scrubbing brush. Let remain until thoroughly dry, then sweep meal out with stiff whisk broom, and let remain in open air until all odor of gasoline escapes

FOR PALMS AND FERNS—A tablespoon of castor oil poured on the ground around the roots of palms and ferns once a month will give them a rapid growth and make them look fresh and green

FOR THE MACHINE—To keep oil from dripping on sewing after oiling, fasten a bit of absorbent cotton to the needle or just above the needle.

TO CLEAN WHITE KID GLOVES—Dip cloth in gasoline and then in prepared chalk, and rub the soiled places on the gloves. Repeat until they are thoroughly clean and you will never again use the old method of putting them on the hands and dipping them in the fluid

KITCHEN HINTS

TO MAKE STEAK TENDER—To transform a tough piece of beefsteak into a nutritious and tender one, by a method employed in many of the first-lass hotels and restaurants, proceed as follows. Put three tablespoons of vinegar into a deep platter, add one of olive oil; lay steak in it for several hours before it is to be used, turning every hour If for breakfast, it should be fixed the night before, steak should be cooked without wiping it and seasoning with butter, pepper and salt and garnished with sliced lemon

FOR JUICY PIE FILLING—A straw, such as is used at soda fountains, cut in two and stood upright in the pie when baking will allow the steam to escape and prevent the juice from running over the edge

BREAKING EGGS—Dip saucer into cold water, before breaking eggs into it, to pour into water to poach and the yolk will not break so easily

TO TENDER MEAT—Tough meat may be made tender by placing in vinegar water for a few minutes.

TO REMOVE ODOR—Biscuit dough, tied in a clean cloth, dropped in boiling cabbage, will do away with all unpleasant odor

TO MAKE PIES BROWN—Take a cloth and wipe the top off with a little sweet milk.

TO IMPROVE ICING—Use one-third teaspoon of cream of tartar.

TO KEEP CAKE FROM FALLING—If you will slam a pan up and down several times, after pouring your cake dough into it, the cake wont fall when you turn it in the stove.

TO KEEP OUT RED ANTS—Place a small quantity of green sage in the pantry shelves

REMEMBER—Slamming the door of the oven makes the cake fall.

TO REMOVE INK STAINS—Rub the stain with ripe tomatoes

TO KEEP LEMON—Cover with cold water, changing every week.

TO KEEP FRUIT OR OTHER CAKE—A ripe apple placed in the cake box will keep it moist and prevent drying out, and retain its freshness.

FOR BURNT FRUITS OR VEGETABLES—When fruit or vegetables burn, set vessel in pan of cold water and remove cover, after a few minutes empty contents into another vessel taking care not to disturb burnt part No burnt taste will remain.

––––––––

TABLE OF WEIGHTS
AND MEASURES

One pint of liquid—One Pound
Two cups of granulated sugar—One Pound
Two and a half cups powdered sugar—One Pound.
Four cups flour—One Quart or One Pound
Two heaping cups butter—One Pound.
Four tablespoonsful—One Wine Glass
Four gills—One pint.
Two tablespoonsful Flour—One ounce
One tablespoon butter—One Ounce. Butter size of an egg—Two Ounces

ENTERTAINMENTS

A NATION CONTEST

1 —What Nation has brought about the most terrible wars? Indig—nation

2.—What nation creates fear and terror? Conster—nation.

8 —What nation exercises the greatest authority? Domi—nation

4 —What nation is very crafty and sly? Machi—nation.

5 —What nation is given over to destruction? Rui—nation.

6 —What nation has produced the most kings? Coro—nation.

7 —What nation did the old prophets come from? Divi—nation.

8 —What nation presents the best men for office? Nomi—nation.

9 —What nation prepares most men for the ministry? Ordi—nation

10 —What nation is the slowest nation? Procrasti—nation.

11 —What nation is famous for its lighting system? Illumi—nation.

12 —What nation is most deluded? Halluci—nation

13 —What nation sees things in a rosy light? Imagi—nation.

14 —What nation is immune from smallpox? Vacci—nation.

15 —What nation produces the most charming people? Fasci—nation

16.—What nation is especially given to voice culture? Into—nation

17—What nation is the most murderous? Assassi—na-
    tion.
18.—What nation is most generous? Do—nation.
19.—What nation is noted for unbridled mirth? Cachin—
    nation.
20—What nation is noted for deep thinking? Rumi—na-
    tion.
21—What nation is growing more youthful? Rejuve—
    nation
22—What nation is the most critical Discrimi—nation
23—What nation is noted for its dullness? Stag—nation
24—What nation has the best actors? Imperso—nation.
25—What nation is most patient and submissive? Resig—
    nation

MECHANICAL TOY PARTY

The invitation said "Bring your favorite mechanical
toy to my house on Saturday evening" This was planned
and carried out by a lad of ten Well, it was wonderful, the
motley array of toys assembled with their owners on a broad
porch of a surburban home one day last week. There were
spiders, beetles, bugs of all kinds. kicking mules, a train
of cars boats that sped across the ocean, forts that blew up
at the right minute, soldiers that went through the man-
ual of arms and of course automobiles that went like the real
ones, and also stopped, and refused to go like real ones One
young hopeful had borrowed his sister's Paris dolls that
lisped her name and said "Mama" and "Papa" like any well
bred child. After the merits of toys had been shown and
discussed the hostess appeared with a luncheon that de-
lighted the boys. There were hard boiled eggs, a fruit salad, sandwiches, crackers and a pink bowl of lemonade to
which they were given free access A party like this is ab-
solutely no trouble as far as entertaining is concerned, for
each guest supplies his own as well as for the others too.

TO DISTRIBUTE CHRISTMAS GIFTS

A novel way to distribute Christmas gifts is to make a huge turkey red stocking, cotton or white drilling. Run a wire in the top of the hem to keep it open, and suspend from a hook in the ceiling by a large red ribbon. Decorate a ladder with ribbon and holly or Christmas green and stand by the stocking. Hang it up a few days before Christmas and drop packages in. Light packages or letters may be pinned on the outside. At breakfast table on Christmas morning draw lots for the honor of unloading the stocking

INDIAN MEAL FOR THANKSGIVING NIGHT

If anyone desires a novelty to which to ask a family of intimate friends, try this on Thanksgiving. Issue your invitation on Indian paper or birch wood paper, asking the guests to come to the Indian Meal. Serve the following menu and have a wigwam for the table centerpiece, with birch bark canoes to hold salted peanuts or popcorn

Corn Mush or Hasty Pudding With Milk
Succotash Bean Soup
Brown Bread or Indian Meal   Corn Bread (Johnny Cake)
Indian Pudding

If the guests will come in Indian costume so much the better. After supper have a bead stringing contest. Use the bright colored beads that come for kindergarten use.

THE GLAD THANKSGIVING TIME

In preparing for Thanksgiving one naturally thinks first of the dinner, but after that happy repast is over and conversation lags there must be something to do, so I am going to tell you about a pumpkin party that would be nice for the evening if you want to ask some children to help celebrate. You may call it a "pumpkin party," for somehow we always associate this gorgeous yellow vegetable with Thanksgiving time So we'll have—

>"Pumpkins large and pumpkins small.
>Pumpkins short and pumpkins tall,
>Pumpkins yellow and pumpkins green,
>Pumpkins dull and those with sheen."

Use one cut in half, lengthwise for the centerpiece (just half.) Fill it with apples, bananas, red grapes and white grapes, purple ones, too, if you can get them Around the top stick Christmas tree candle holders and fill with small white candles When lit the effect is lovely, and as pretty a centerpiece as you can imagine. Yellow crepe paper may be fashioned into adorable pumpkins for holding salted nuts, and the light may be shaded with paper pumpkin blossoms. Have a huge paper pumpkin for a "Jack Horner" pie, with yellow ribbons, one for each child For favors you may use popcorn put up like ears of corn in green oiled paper with green paper corn leaves For this informal occasion I would suggest using the pretty "Thanksgiving" paper napkins, and if you do not mind extra trouble each child may have a yellow crepe paper pumpkin cap to wear Serve very simple "eats" consisting of cold turkey sandwiches, cocoa, popcorn, molasses candy and wee pumpkin tarts with a spoonful of ice cream on top.

A HOLIDAY PARTY

Here is how a holiday party was given once upon a time not so very long ago. It was a white affair, with quantities of silver decorations, which were lovely The invitations were on heavy white paper ornamented with wreaths in silver tinsel and holly wreaths tied with red ribbon and silver gauze. The combination was lovely The lamps were shaded with white and silver and the candle shades for the table were of white and silver

The first game was a pretty one, a large wreath of frosted holly leaves was suspended by silver cords, in the center was a cluster of silvered sleigh bells Each guest was handed three white rubber balls and allowed three throws at the bells. If any throw made the bells jingle a prize of a silver paper box of silver wrapped bon-bons was awarded

Guests Blindfolded

Then a silver-leaved wreath was laid flat upon the table containing a number of white candles The guests were blindfolded and the one who succeeded in blowing out the largest number of candles at one blow was given a pretty box tied with silver cord which said "For a Blower," and was found to contain a handkerchief In this game the prizes were the same for the boy and the girl.

The dining room table was a thing of beauty; it was first covered with cotton, sprinkled with quantities of diamond dust, the edge of the table outlined with silver leaves, and the same leaves surrounded the plates A small gift tree was in the center, trimmed entirely in white and silver, with red electric lights. Just imagine how pretty it all looked The place cards were frosted silver and white bells and were hung from the tumblers by silver-paper birds. A large white cake with red candles was cut with ceremony and favors of silver were found inside for the guests.

AN ANNOUNCEMENT PARTY

This was given in the evening, and both men and women were asked. There were about 20 guests, all good friends, so the affair was not at all stiff The hostess passed cards tied with true-lover's knots of blue with little blueprints (snapshots) of the happy pair at the top. Below the word "Matrimony" was printed in blue and gold letters. The game was to see how many words (proper names barred) could be made in half-hour.

Every one was surprised at the announcement, which was told without any other explanation, and the couple were overwhelmed with congratulations.

At the conclusion of the word contest a basket was passed containing tiny bells, wee slippers, two rings, two hearts, envelopes containing a love message, etc. Thus partners were found by matching these love tokens. Then to the music of Lohengrin's wedding march, they went to the dining room, where this dainty repast was served: Creamed chicken in heart-shaped patties, hot biscuits, also heart-shaped; ambrosia, and pink-iced heart cakes; "Lover's delight" nectar was served in tall glasses. This was merely grape juice with plenty of cracked ice.

A HAPPINESS LUNCHEON

For a recent bride a Bluebird Luncheon was given by her maid of honor and attended by her most intimate girl friends.

The usual white table linen was dispensed with and one of the blue and white Japanese cloths used. The design was one of bluebirds skimming across the white ground. The napkins matched the cloth, and blue white dishes were used. The centerpiece was a cut glass bowl filled with bride roses and bachelor-buttons. From the chandelier overhead were suspended bluebirds by invisible threads, so that they fluttered gracefully over the bowl of flowers. These the hostess made by drawing the birds on cardboard, painting them in the proper tints, and cutting them out. The same birds formed the place cards and were poised on the edge of the water glasses, bearing in their bills the names of the guests.

There was no attempt, of course, to carry out the decorative idea in the menu; but with the coffee each guest gave a "happiness toast" to the bride-to-be. These had been prepared beforehand at the request of the hostess, who had sent to each girl a bluebird decorated card on which her toast was to be written and brought to the luncheon. Many of the toasts were original, but some were quotations from the play "The Bluebird."

In the afternoon, games were played and the prizes were bits of jewelry in the popular bluebird design, the guest favor being a quaint silver necklace with pendant of an enameled bluebird, from all the girls.

APPENDIX

BOUILLON—Take four pounds of lean beef and cut in small pieces and boil in four quarts of water, let cook slowly for four or five hours until reduced to two quarts. Remove from fire and let cool with meat in the liquor. Then squeeze all moisture from meat and let stand all night. Next morning skim off all grease and place upon the fire Whip the white of an egg to a stiff froth and stir in the boiling liquid, so as to collect all impurities. After boiling a few minutes remove skim and strain. Season with salt and pepper, serve hot with a slice or little block of lemon.

CHICKEN CROQUETTES—One solid cup of meat chopped fine, season with one-half teaspoon of salt, one half teaspoon celery salt, one salt spoon of pepper and a speck of cayenne, a few drops of onion juice, one tablespoon lemon juice, one teaspoon chopped parsley. Mix with a thick sauce made with two tablespoonfuls of butter, two of flour, one cup of milk Spread on plate and let cool, shape and roll in cracker meal and egg and fry. This makes about twelve. It is better to make one day and fry the next

BAKED BASS OR TROUT—Take one nice trout or bass, weighing about four pounds, dress and place on ice for a short time, remove from ice and place in long pan, rub with salt and a small quantity of black pepper,, pour just enough water over the fish to keep it from burning, and add about one heaping tablespoon of Crisco, set in stove and let cook for about 30 minutes, have ready a dressing made from two cups bread crumbs, one tablespoon butter, small onion chopped fine, just enough to slightly taste, two pieces of celery, also chopped fine or celery seed may be used, black pepper, and salt to season, one dozen small fresh oysters and mix with the water from where the fish is cooked, fill fish with this dressing and also place around fish in the pan, return to stove add more hot water if needed, and bake until done, but not fall to pieces. Serve on platter that has been heated, garnish with sliced lemon. The liquor from this makes all sauce necessary for gravy, as the dressing thickens it to a creamy gravy

Be sure in dressing fish to bake to leave the head on but remove eyes and gills This is an attractive dish and also one very much relished

FRIED LAKE TROUT—SOUTHERN STYLE—Take fresh game fish, small trout are best, dress and place on ice till ready to cook. Have a deep frying pan or pot, fill with lard or frying fat to about one half its depth, let come to a lively boil, salt fish and dip in meal and drop into the boiling fat, keep hot and when brown on one side turn and repeat this until the fish is done but do not allow to cook till hard. Serve while hot with sliced lemon. Large trout have to be sliced in halves before cooking but the small ones are fine cooked whole

SCALLOPED OYSTERS—Take amount of oysters, put a layer in pan, then a layer of rolled crackers, butter and milk, pepper and salt until pan is full then run in stove and brown, cook about half hour.

IRISH POTATO AU GRATIN WITH PIMENTOES—Boil potatoes in dice form until tender, take off stove and arrange in pan with layer of potatoes then a layer of grated cheese with little dabs of pimento about over the cheese, then another layer of potatoes, cheese, etc, season with salt and pepper as you go on then make a cream dressing and put over the top with cheese sprinkled over that and dabs of pimento, put in stove and brown

CREAM DRESSING—One cup sweet milk, heaping teaspoon of sifted flour, pinch of salt and black pepper, one spoonful butter, cook until thick, put over the potatoes and brown. Make a larger quantity if needed.

CORN RELISH—Chop with a knife one half large cabbage, two bunches celery. Run through meat chopper, 3 large onions, 4 1-2 red bell peppers, 4 1-2 green bell peppers,1 green hot pepper, 2 red hot peppers. Take one-half box mustard, 1 pound sugar, 1-3 cup salt, 1 qt. of white vinegar, 1 tablespoon tumeric; cook until light brown color then add ten ears of tender corn, cut and scraped, and cook a little longer, this will make nine quarts. If more is wanted double recipe

SWEET POTATOES WITH MARSHMALLOWS—Boil whole potatoes until done, then peel and mash, add sweet milk, a pinch of salt, a tablespoon of butter, sugar enough to sweeten to taste, a little nutmeg or cinnamon. In using the milk use just enough to make the potatoes a smooth paste. Add one or two whole eggs well beaten put in pan and bake until a nice even brown Just before serving cover with marshmallows set in oven and brown slightly. Be careful not to get the potatoes too soft or they will not be so good

SCALLOPED IRISH POTATOES—Peel potatoes and slice round thin slices, put layer in a pan, then a layer of milk and little lumps of butter and sprinkle flour between each layer and salt and pepper to taste, put tiny little onion between each layer, fix several layers and then run in stove until cooked and brown.

CHOCOLATE PIE—Two and one-half cups sweet milk, two pinches of salt, one-half cup of cocoa dissolved in hot water, yolks of three eggs, put right in milk and beat all up together, about one and one-half cups sugar or sweeten to taste, one spoon butter, three heaping tablespoons of sifted flour, set on stove and stir constantly until thick. Bake crusts and let all cool and about half an hour before meals, put filling into crusts and make meringue of whites by beating stiff and adding one heaping tablespoon of sugar to each egg. Put over pies and brown This makes two pies. Flavor with vanilla

DELICIOUS MINCE PIE—Take one small box of mince meat, put in boiler and add enough water to dissolve and make mince meat soft, add three tablespoons of sugar and cook until the right thickness for pies Line pie plate with crust and fill in with the mince meat, cover top with layer of crust and prick with fork, bake to a nice smooth brown—serve smoking hot with whipped cream and black coffee.

BANANA SHORT CAKE—Make a rich pie crust. Roll very thin and cook in bottom of biscuit pan, prick with fork, cook slowly till crisp. Bake three or four layers, when ready to serve slice bananas very thin and put a layer between crusts and on top, sprinkle a little sugar on each layer. Serve with caramel sauce

CARAMEL SAUCE—Take two cups of sugar, two tablespoonfuls of dry flour mixed in one cup of sugar, one tablespoon of butter, two cups water Then take the other cup of sugar and put in a skillet and let melt slowly, stir continually until melted and browned Put first part in stew pan to itself and let come to boil, then add the brown part and stir until smooth Take off, strain and flavor with vanilla.

ORANGE CAKE—Four tablespoons butter, one cup sugar two-thirds cup milk, one egg, two cups flour, four teaspoons Royal Baking Powder, one-eighth teaspoon salt, one teaspoon orange extract, grated rind of one orange. Cream butter, add sugar slowly, beating well, add milk a little at a time, then add well beaten egg. Sift dry ingredients together and add to the mixture, add flavoring and grated orange rind and mix well. Bake in a greased shallow cake tin in a hot oven for fifteen or twenty minutes When cool cut with fancy cutter and cover with orange icing Can be baked in individual cake tins if desired.

ORANGE ICING—Two cupfuls confectioners sugar, two tablespoons boiling water, two teaspoons lemon juice, grated rind of one orange, and a little orange pulp if desired. Add water slowly to the sugar to make a smooth paste, add flavoring and grated rind of one orange and spread on the cake.

OATMEAL COOKIES—Two cups of raw oatmeal, two cups flour, one cup sugar, one cup of lard or butter, two eggs, one cup chopped nuts, one scant teaspoon soda in four tablespoons of butter milk. One heaping teaspoon of cinnamon, pinch of salt, vanilla to taste. Make size of walnut and drop on buttered pans one inch apart. Bake ten or fifteen minutes in a moderate oven

DOUGHNUTS—Four cups of sifted flour, three level teaspoons of Royal Baking Powder, one-half teaspoon of salt, one cup of sugar, two eggs beaten together, two tablespoons of melted butter, one cup of milk; sift flour, then measure; add baking powder and salt and sift three times; rub sugar and butter together; add well beaten eggs, then flour and milk alternately; turn out on a well floured board and roll out one-half inch thick, cut with doughnut cutter and fry in boiling fat; flavor with vanilla or cinnamon.

TARTAR SAUCE—To one cup of mayonnaise dressing add one small finely chopped onion, one tablespoon each of finely chopped capers, sweet gherkins and olives, and one-half tablespoon each finely chopped parsley and fresh tarragon. Mix well and keep cool until ready to serve

VIENNAISE SAUCE—Reduce one small can of tomatoes by slow cooking to a thick pulp. When strained there should be two tablespoonsful. To 2-4 of cup of mayonnaise dressing add 3-4 tablespoon of finely chopped capers, one teaspoon finely chopped parsley, two teaspoons each finely chopped gherkins and olives, one teaspoon finely chopped onion. Add tomato pulp, mix well and keep in a cool place.

THOUSAND ISLE DRESSING—One half pint of mayonnaise, two hard boiled eggs chopped fine, a small piece of onion chopped fine, and two medium sized beets chopped fine after being cooked. One light teaspoon of sugar, one 1-2 cup of tomato catsup, mix thoroughly and keep in a cool place

CRANBERRY SAUCE—Take cranberries, wash and pick them put amount of cranberries in vessel on stove with a little water over them, enough to cover, let boil until tender, then put sugar enough to sweeten to taste, then let boil until the mixture begins to jelly in a saucer when tried; then take up and rub through a sieve into the bowl they will be served in Let stand all night and it will be hard.

LEMON SAUCE—One cup sugar, one egg well beaten into sugar, one cup water, juice and rind one lemon, lump of butter size of an egg, place on stove to cook after stirring in two tablespoons of corn starch or flour, let boil and serve as sauce over plain cake This is delicious if made right.

CHICKEN ASPIC—Boil one large hen as for salad and cut into small pieces with a pair of scissors. Place a layer of chicken in a flat pan and arrange on this a layer of hard boiled eggs cut in circles then a layer of pecans and celery cut fine, until all chicken in used Place liquor in which chicken was boiled back on stove and cook down to one quart Add one heaping tablespoon of gelatine, juice of two lemons, salt, and black and cayenne pepper, pour over contents of pan when it is just beginning to congeal, cut in slices and serve with mayonnaise

TOMATO ASPIC—Two tablespoons gelatine, one half cup cold water, three and half cups tomato juice, one egg, hard boiled, cayenne pepper to taste, 2 cloves, one tablespoon of good vinegar, salt to taste, three medium sized whole fresh tomatoes

Soak gelatine in cold water till dissolved Cook tomato juice, add seasoning except vinegar and boil ten minutes. Add vinegar and soaked gelatine and strain. Cut egg and tomatoes in rings and dip in gelatine and arrange in sides and bottom of bowl or mold. Add gelatine slowly, allowing it to set gradually, so egg and tomato will not fall out of place Place on ice till ready to serve. Cut in slices, place on lettuce leaf and serve with stiff mayonnaise This makes a pretty salad to serve at card parties.

CARROT SALAD—Take one bunch of carrots and peel and grate Peel and cut into dice shape six apples and a small bunch of celery, mix in some pecan nuts; mix the whole together with mayonnaise, serve on lettuce leaf with mayonnaise on top This is fine.

IRISH POTATO SALAD—Cut potatoes in dice, put in vessel and salt to taste, cook slowly till just done. When cold cut up celery in it and a tiny bit of onion. Mix with mayonnaise, serve on lettuce leaf.

RAINBOW SALAD—Two slices of pineapple, a ring of green and a ring of red bell pepper or pimento, a few chopped nuts, two cheese balls, top with stiff whipped cream or mayonnaise, and dot with cherries, one green and one red, serve on crisp lettuce leaves. This is a pretty salad at any time

FRUIT WINE—One pound raisins, 1 pound prunes, 1 pound evaporated peaches, 3 pounds sugar, 1 gallon water, one Fleischman s Yeast Cake Let stand one month and strain up.

BAKED GRITS—Take a dish of cold grits, mix up with sweet milk and two eggs, one tablespoon of flour, one of butter, work until all lumps are out and it is a nice smooth batter thicker than for batter cakes, then brown in a pan and grate cheese over the top. This has to cook about half an hour before putting the cheese on.

ICES—Orange sherbert to be served with the orange cake. One cup orange juice, juice of one lemon, two cups of sugar, five cups water. Grate rind of two oranges and rub into the sugar. Add water and boil three minutes. Strain through a cheese cloth. Dissolve in the sugar and water one package of lemon or unflavored Jell-O Ice Cream Powder. Add juice of orange and lemon, and one large can of grated pineapple, freeze and serve. Makes about three quarts. A section of orange on top adds to the beauty of this ice.

HEAVENLY JAM—Six pounds of blue grapes, five pounds of sugar, four oranges, one pound raisins. Take the grapes and squeeze the pulp out and put into separate pan and cook pulp until all seeds come out, stirring all of the time to keep from sticking. Chop hulls of grapes real fine, also cut up the raisins. Grate the rind of the four oranges. Then take the orange pulp out of the skin with a knife or fruit spoon and put all together and cook for thirty minutes. This will make eight pints and is delicious.

A PRETTY CHRISTMAS DINNER

Have dining room all decorated in red and green holly. Arrange table with a pretty center of red and green. Take large red apples polished as favors. Cut off one end and scoop out the inside. Fill each apple with nuts and candy. Place one apple on one side of plate for each person, in nest of holly. Then take three or four crackers and place together and tie a red ribbon around to hold in place with a little bow at one corner and a sprig of holly and berries at opposite corner making a box, fill this box with chicken salad and place box on a little plate with lettuce leaf at opposite corner, apple also in a nest of holly. Serve turkey with cranberry sauce and dressing filled with oysters. Hot rice, asparagus loaf, creamed English peas. Hot biscuits or sliced bread. Sweet peach pickle. Dessert, orange sponge served with fruit cake made by tried and tested recipe in this book

SUGGESTED MENUS

———

Sunday Dinner

Chicken Consomme with Whipped Cream. (p. 3)
Fride Chicken, Southern Style, Cream Gravy (p. 9).
Rice.   Potatoes au gratin with Pimentoes (p. 105).
Asparagus on toast (p. 26).   English Peas with cream
dressing in pastry cups. (p. 105).
Hot Biscuits (p. 21).
Fruit Salad. (p. 61) on lettuce leaf with whipped cream.
Orange Pudding (p. 32)   Orange Cake (p. 57).
Coffee.   Whipped Cream.

Sunday Supper

Thinly Sliced Boiled Ham. Thousand Isle Dressing (p. 109).
Stuffed Eggs on Lettuce (p. 74).
Tomato sandwiches (p. 30).
Irish Potato Salad (p. 110).
Thinly sliced bread.
Preserves.
Coffee.   Tea

Monday Breakfast

Grape Fruit or Oranges
Oatmeal.
Toast Bacon
Eggs, as preferred
Hot Flannel Cakes (p. 20).
Syrup
Coffee.   Tea.

Monday Dinner

Veal Loaf (p 74).   Tomato Sauce (p 58)
Green String Beans (p. 24)
Squash, Mexican style (p. 24)
Creamed Irish Potatoes baked brown
Candied Yams, Southern Style.   Cornbread Muffins (p. 19).
Apple Roll (p. 41) with hard sauce, (p 58)
Coffee   Tea

Monday Supper

Broiled Steak (p 7) French fried potatoes (p 26).
Hot Grits
Scrambled Eggs   Hot Muffins (p 19)
Coffee.

Tuesday Breakfast

Corn Flakes with Bananas and Pure Cream
Toast   Broiled Ham
Eggs cooked as preferred
Fried Apples.
Hot Flannel Cakes (p 20)   Syrup
Hot Coffee   Tea

Tuesday Dinner

Stuffed Roast with Dressing (p 10)
Cabbage, Cream Dressing, Sliced Eggs   Spaghetti with To-
matoes and Onions (p. 72).
Creamed Irish potatoes
Baked sweet potatoes
Sliced tomatoes.   Mayonnaise (p. 59).
Banana Short Cake (p 107)   Caramel Sauce (p 107).

Tuesday Supper

Pork Sausage with Fried Sweet Potatoes (p 26).
Hit Grits
Cored Baked Apples in peel, with Whipped Cream (p 38).
Egg Omelet (p. 72)   Hot Biscuits (p 19)

—113—

Wednesday Dinner

Baked Chicken, Dressing (p. 9).   Hot Rice.
Scalloped Irish potatoes (p. 106).
Sweet potatoes with marshmallows (p. 106)
Pear Salad.   Lettuce.   Mayonnaise (p. 62).
Hot Biscuits (p. 19).
Japanese Cake (p 53)   Orange Jello (p. 37).
Coffee.   Tea.

Wednesday Supper.

Oyster Soup (p. 3)
Ham. Eggs, straight up and turned, mingled on dish with
ham.   Rice or Grits.
Cheese Souffle (p. 70).
Irish Potato Chips (p. 25).
Hot Biscuits (p. 19).
Coffee   Tea.

Thursday Breakfast

Oranges.   Cream of Wheat with pure cream.
Toast.   Breakfast Bacon
Brains and Eggs.
Waffles (p. 19).
Coffee.   Tea

Thursday Dinner

Vegetable soup with crackers (p. 5).
Pork Roast Southern style with sweet potatoes peeled and
baked around it (p. 11).
English Peas, with Eggs a la English (p. 75).
Spaghetti and Cheese (p 72).   Spinach with Eggs (p. 25).
Corn bread muffins (p. 19).
Banana Salad served on lettuce leaves with Mayon-
naise (p. 62).
Lemon Pie (p. 43)   Coffee.   Tea.

—114—

Thursday Supper.

Steak fried French style (p. 7).
Smothered Eggs on Toast (p. 73).
Baked grits with grated cheese on top (p. 110).
Stuffed Irish Potatoes (p. 25).
Hot Biscuits (p. 21), or Muffins (p. 19).
Coffee   Tea.

Friday Breakfast.

Orange. Oatmeal or any cereal with cream.
Toast. Fried green tomatoes (p. 27).
Bacon and eggs.
Hot cakes (p. 20), with syrup.
Coffee,   Tea,

Friday Dinner.

Red Snapper, Creole style (p. 15). Creamed Irish potatoes.
Stuffed Bell Peppers (p. 27).
Carrot Salad (p. 110).
Corn Muffins (p. 19). Baked Sweet Potatoes.
Chocolate Pie (p. 44).   Coffee.   Tea.

Friday Supper.

Scalloped Oysters (p. 105).   Spanish Omelet (p. 77). Grits.
Cheese Straws (p. 72).
French Fried Potatoes (p. 26).
Hot Biscuits (p. 21).
Coffee.   Tea.

Saturday Breakfast

Shredded Biscuit, toasted with Peaches and Cream.
Breakfast Bacon. Toast with Eggs on top.
Hot Flannel Cakes (p. 20).
Coffee.   Tea.

Saturday Dinner

Creole Steak. Creamed Irish Potatoes (p. 28).
Sweet Potatoes in pan (p. 26). Stuffed Egg Plant (p. 28).
Spaghetti and Cheese (p. 72).
Tomatoes and Mayonnaise (p. 59).
Chocolate Pudding with Sauce (p. 33).

Saturday Supper

Boiled Salmon with sauce (p. 16). Spoon Bread (p. 19).
Goulash (p. 14). Irish potato chips (p. 25).
Quick Rolls (p. 21).
Coffee   Tea.

Second Sunday Dinner

Almond Bisque.
Chicken Pie (p. 9). Rice.
Cauliflower (p. 25).
Sweet Potato Pone (p. 26). Mushrooms with English Peas.
Stuffed Tomato Salad (p. 63), on Lettuce Leaf.
Sliced Light Bread or hot Biscuit.
Marshmallow Pudding (p. 33). Whipped Cream White Loaf
Cake (p. 48).

Second Wednesday Supper

Oyster Cocktail (p. 16).
Creole Chicken with Sauce (p. 13).
Cheese Balls in Rice Nests (p. 70). Scrambled Eggs.
Hot Biscuits (p. 21).
Apple Tapioca Pudding (p. 37).   Coffee.   Tea.

TABLE OF CONTENTS

———

THE YAZOO CITY HERALD PRINT
YAZOO CITY, MISS.
1922

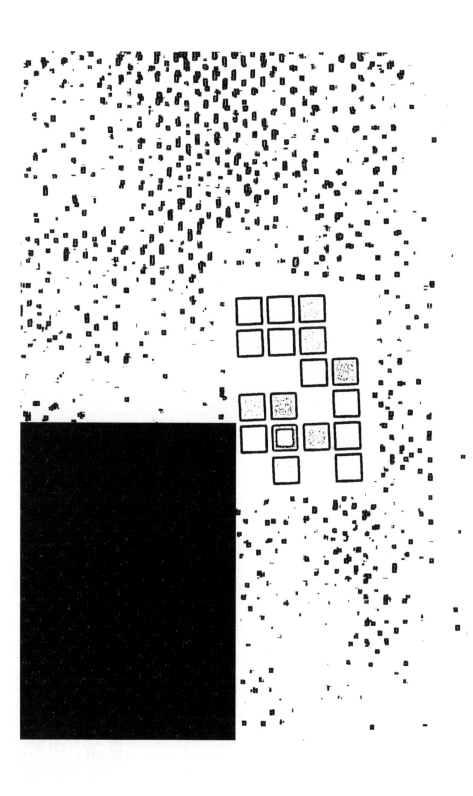

Lightning Source UK Ltd.
Milton Keynes UK
UKHW020635180321
380569UK00005B/421